Drama

as a Way of Knowing

PAUL G. HELLER

 Stenhouse Publishers

 The Galef Institute

Strategies for Teaching and Learning Professional Library

Administrators: Supporting School Change by Robert Wortman
Assessment: Continuous Learning by Lois Bridges
Creating Your Classroom Community by Lois Bridges
Drama as a Way of Knowing by Paul G. Heller
Math as a Way of Knowing by Susan Ohanian
Music as a Way of Knowing by Nick Page

Look for announcements of future titles in this series on dance, second language learners, literature, physical education, science, visual arts, and writing.

Stenhouse Publishers, 431 York Street, York, Maine 03909
The Galef Institute, 11050 Santa Monica Boulevard, Third Floor, Los Angeles, California 90025

Library of Congress Cataloging-in-Publication Data
Heller, Paul G.
    Drama as a way of knowing : strategies for teaching and learning professional library / Paul G. Heller.
      p.   cm.
    Simultaneously published: Los Angeles, Calif. : Galef Institute. c1995.
    Includes bibliographical references.
    ISBN 1-57110-050-4 (alk. paper)
    1. Drama in education.   I. Title.
PN3171.H3346 1996
371.3'32—dc20
                                            96-45739
                                          CIP

Manufactured in the United States of America on acid-free paper
01 00 99 98 97 96 8 7 6 5 4 3 2 1

Dear Colleague,

This is an exciting time for us to be educators.

Research across disciplines informs our understanding of human learning and development. We know how to support students as active, engaged learners in our classrooms. We know how to continuously assess student learning and development to make sensitive, instructional decisions. This is the art of teaching—knowing how to respond effectively at any given moment to our students' developmental needs.

As educators, we know that learning the art of teaching takes time, practice, and lots of professional support. To that end, the Strategies for Teaching and Learning Professional Library was developed. Each book invites you to explore theory (to know why) in the context of exciting teaching strategies (to know how) connected to evaluation of your students' learning as well as your own (to know you know). In addition, you'll find in-depth information about the unique rigors and challenges of each discipline, to help you make the most of the rich learning and teaching opportunities each discipline offers.

> Use the books' *Dialogues* on your own and in the study groups to reflect upon your practices. The Dialogues invite responses to self-evaluative questions, experimentation with new instructional strategies in classrooms, and perhaps a rethinking of learning philosophy and classroom practices stimulated by new knowledge and understanding.

> *Shoptalks* offer you lively reviews of the best and latest professional literature including professional journals and associations.

> *Teacher-To-Teacher Field Notes* are full of tips and experiences from practicing educators who offer different ways of thinking about teaching practices and a wide range of classroom strategies they've found practical and successful.

As you explore and reflect on teaching and learning, we believe you'll continue to refine and extend your teaching art, and enjoy your professional life and the learning lives of your students.

Here's to the art of teaching!

Lois Bridges
Professional Development Editorial Director,
The Galef Institute

The Strategies for Teaching and Learning Professional Library is part of the Galef Institute's school reform initiative *Different Ways of Knowing.*

Different Ways of Knowing is a philosophy of education based on research in child development, cognitive theory, and multiple intelligences. It offers teachers, administrators, specialists, and other school and district educators continuing professional growth opportunities integrated with teaching and learning materials. The materials are supportive of culturally and linguistically diverse school populations and help all teachers and children to be successful. Teaching strategies focus on interdisciplinary, thematic instruction integrating history and social studies with the performing and visual arts, literature, writing, math, and science. Developed with the leadership of Senior Author Linda Adelman, *Different Ways of Knowing* has been field tested in hundreds of classrooms across the country.

For more information, write or call

The Galef Institute
11050 Santa Monica Boulevard, Third Floor, Los Angeles, California 90025
Tel 310.479.8883
Fax 310.473.9720

Strategies for Teaching and Learning Professional Library

Contributors

President
Linda Adelman

Vice President Programs and Communications
Sue Beauregard

Professional Development Editorial Director
Lois Bridges

Editor
Resa Gabe Nikol

Editorial Assistants
Elizabeth Finison, Wendy Sallin

Designers
Melvin Harris, Delfina Marquez-Noé, Sarah McCormick, Jennifer Swan Myers, Julie Suh

Photographers
Ted Beauregard, Dana Ross

This book is dedicated with grateful thanks to Suzanne James-Peters and her third-grade class, and to Cheryl Nelson and her first-grade class at Mary Farmar Elementary School in Benicia, California. These creative teachers and children were essential in helping me to describe how young children learn through play, rehearsal, and performance. I would also like to express my appreciation to Mary Farmar school principal, Jane West, for inviting me to visit.

And I thank Drama Specialist Christine Caton who so generously lent her professional knowledge, insights, and writing to the creation of this text. —PGH

Special thanks to Andrew G. Galef and Bronya Pereira Galef for their continuing commitment to our nation's children and educators.

Contents

Chapter 1

The Stuff of Drama

*Eeeeeck, drama, yikes, it's so much work, it's so...so...noisy and exhaust-
ing, and disorganized. Couldn't I just avoid it?*

Nope.

It's here already. It's entered your classroom. It's inside your students. It explodes every minute. Admit it: your class is a major melodrama. There's the stuff of drama in our lives every day: sounds full of portent like church bells ringing, confusing street noises, people shouting, or couples whispering secrets. Just driving to work, we see people all alone in their cars performing monologues by singing, ranting, or talking on the phone. Every day we make dramatic discoveries about other people, or they reveal something new and theatrical about themselves to us. Our lives are filled with the same things we pay to see in plays: dramatic tension, conflict, odd characters, hidden objects, death, love, and mystery. Check out the newspapers and magazines. There's drama and theater right there before our eyes. We read about it, watch it on television, and are drawn into watching it unfold time and time again.

When people recreate events, they are playing. If the recreating is informal, we might call it just plain play. But, if it's a formal recreating, we call it a play. Both are happening in your classroom every day.

Recreating events in play or a play has been very important to all peoples since the dawn of humankind. Cave men recreated or reenacted hunts in ceremonies to ensure success during future hunts. Religious people today celebrate by recreating past events during holidays and other special days. Throughout time, strolling players, jugglers, acrobats, vaudeville artists, clowns, mimes, and actors have fascinated people. (Sometimes when entertainers recreated life too well—especially political life, they were censored.) The point is that we humans like to watch ourselves through actors on stage.

Ninety percent of the success of drama in a classroom is based on just this idea: we're fascinated by watching other people perform. It is this fascination that will make drama riveting in your classroom. So check this out: If something truly dramatic happens in your classroom—an altercation, a major spill, a very loud noise—doesn't everything stop and everyone pay attention to what just happened? Sure. You wish they wouldn't; you wish the students would concentrate on their math work, but you and math are no match for the theatrical spectacle that just took place. So, one reason to involve drama as an aid to learning is to focus the students' attention on something they and you consider important and intrinsically interesting.

The best time to read this book is when you have decided what kinds of things you would like your students to learn about, and you would like to offer them a dramatic way to show what they have learned, how they have integrated what they know with newly acquired knowledge, and how they apply knowledge to new situations.

To Bring Drama into Your Class, You Hardly Have To Move a Muscle
Try answering the Dialogue questions on the next page. For the purposes of this Dialogue, let's define drama as the general kinds of acting you're most familiar with and that this book deals with: pantomiming, improvising, and rehearsed scene production—what you would see on a television sitcom or soap opera, or in a theatrical production.

The best time to use drama in your classroom is when you wish students to

- engage in the process of feeling, physically and emotionally, what it is like to be someone or something
- make creative and artistic choices about how they use and present what they have learned
- show an audience what these experiences were like—to create empathy, understanding, discussion, and so on
- predict outcomes, make hypotheses, synthesize knowledge, account for ambiguity, and engage in a range of higher level critical thinking.

DIALOGUE

Consider these examples. Then respond to questions about student learning in your classroom.

Class A studies the frog and its muscular structure.
Class B studies the frog and its muscular structure *and*, as an activity integral to their learning, they act out the leg actions of a frog. What new information would Class B gather that Class A wouldn't?

_____

_____

_____

Here's another example to think about. Consider the difference in learning between Class A—who studied the way our body breaks down proteins, and Class B—who studied the same information and then acted that process out. What would Class A be missing?

_____

_____

_____

What could my students learn by acting out some of the processes, procedures, or events of my next science learning event?

_____

_____

_____

When we watch a performance of *Romeo and Juliet*, we are really watching actors who have researched what it was like to live in Italy hundreds of years ago. The actors have also researched the way people express their emotions about passionate love and hate. Then, in rehearsal, they practice feeling what it is like to be these people and to express the characters' emotions through thought, action, and voice.

Performances in the classroom give youngsters the same opportunities for learning. The activities in this book encourage students to play a scientist of the future, Billy the Kid, a pan of gold found in the Klondike, wolves, or the Himalayas. The processes are the same as for an actor playing Juliet. The students explore or research location and time and what these people, places, or things feel (or felt) like. Then they can make choices about how thought, action, and voice will reveal their findings. In this way, drama in the classroom becomes a way for students to develop intimacy, sympathy, and above all empathy for other people and things.

The Work Load

Drama is hard work if you do for the students what they can do for themselves. If you write the scripts, make the costumes and scenery, or worry about making it snow indoors, you could be up all night for weeks. But the great thing about drama is that students can create and manipulate every aspect of it. Realizing this is the first step to making drama easy and fun.

What makes drama easy is that you don't have to model it yourself. If you enjoy acting, pantomiming, and writing, and your doing so enhances the quality of your teaching, then by all means act in the classroom, model the activities, and participate as much as you want. Personally, I've never found that my students did much better when I modeled a role or method for them. When they had to develop the role, or figure out the actions to pantomime a scene, or look in the mirror to get their facial expressions right, they were learning to depend on themselves. That process, no matter what the production looked like, was valuable and rewarding to them (and to me). As teachers, we are professionals trained to make suggestions, provide information when needed, and to encourage. If we're doing that, then we can leave the acting to the students.

You don't have to worry if the student actors are good or bad by the standards of "Masterpiece Theater," Laurence Olivier, or by some other criteria that comes to mind. I'm not suggesting that students don't have a sense of how well or badly they have acted, it's just that such standards are not what drama in the classroom is all about. Classroom drama is primarily about learning and synthesizing knowledge; not judging performance, honing the craft of acting, or winning auditions, roles, and Oscars. Later on I'll discuss some guidelines that will help students evaluate their performances based on what they learned rather than what they thought was good or bad acting.

Drama activities are active and interactive ways for students to show what they know, process current lessons, and integrate new knowledge with other disciplines.

You can tailor the drama activities specifically for your students and your classroom. I'll suggest some possibilities, but in the Dialogue sections of this book, I'll help you to write the type of drama activities that will be best for your students. After you give the prompt, watch your students learn! Drama activities are active and interactive ways for students to show what they know, process current lessons, and integrate new knowledge with other disciplines. Since drama is 100 percent active, there's little down time. Eventually students are talking about the scene they'll do, writing about it, improvising it, rehearsing it, and performing it. At each stage, they have to take into account thousands of facts and make decisions about movement—all the while *thinking*. Your job is not to manage or regulate them, but to watch them learn, set guidelines, facilitate, and make suggestions.

Teaching via drama is nonintrusive. "What would happen if..." are the words beginning most of my questions to my students when I'm about to spring a new movement or concept on them. If you see something that simply isn't working, explain the problem and ask for solutions.

Your students' work will amuse you. It will make you laugh, and amaze you.

DIALOGUE

Let's consider again how students can deepen their under-
standings through drama.

What would students learn if, while studying exploration, for
example, they acted out what the continent of America felt like
to the Europeans the first time they set foot on it? What might
they learn about exploration that they wouldn't learn by
reading only?

_____

_____

_____

_____

Drama Is Educationally Sound

Research shows that drama does enhance learning. You could have predicted
that, right? When we cry at movies or become engaged by action in a stage
performance, or we're aching to dance because a live band is so hot, all of
that is responding to ourselves and learning about our emotions. When students act, they learn about themselves by working with others, and then facing the audience and actually performing; it's about the most honest moment
people experience. It's live and it's terrifying sometimes, and it's soooo much
fun. That in itself is pretty good evidence that drama in the classroom is
educationally sound, but I thought you might be interested in how drama
pedagogically enhances learning.

First of all, on the most basic of levels, we all know that students learn by
seeing, _and_ by hearing, _and_ by doing. In a full instructional environment,
students can typically grasp concepts after eight repetitions of various types
of learning. For example, if the students are studying water pollution, they
might do any one or a combination of the following activities:

- watch a demonstration about industrial waste
- do an experiment in which they "pollute" a dish of water
- read an article about the effect of waste on healthy cells
- answer questions about what they read
- write a journal entry about what they have done and observed

- share their findings in group work
- contact local government agencies with a letter about their concerns
- pantomime the effect of a specific toxin on water.

So, just in terms of a complement to other modes of instruction, drama makes a lot of sense.

Secondly, drama activities help transform school from a place where we tell students what to think to a place where we help them experience thinking. The majority of thinking for drama entails analysis, synthesis, and evaluation.

Field Notes: Teacher-To-Teacher

A number of my acting students were accidently turning their backs to the audience. To solve this problem, I asked them to break up into pairs and to do a scene in which they both faced the audience. One student was to stand behind the other, and I directed the actor in front never to turn around, but to listen to the actor behind and react with face, body, and voice directly to someone in the audience. I was trying to show the actors that on stage it is fine to react to someone without actually facing them. This would look very odd in real life, but because the audience is in front, actors have to learn to include them in their facial and body movements. Everyone did well. In their next presentations, all my students faced the audience and acted with perfection. Well…that's not exactly true. Only three of them faced the audience the next time. Okay, it was only one student out of thirty-four.

But the point I'm trying to make is that one person improved, and soon there were two or three. Six weeks later, ten students kept their faces to the audience. My students and I have until June to learn how to do this.

So, relax. Nothing here has to be accomplished overnight. Some of your students will immediately understand the activities, and how the activities help them learn and express their knowledge; some of your students will take weeks or months to learn and feel comfortable with this. But the process is the key to learning, and thinking about it is important.

—PGH

Drama activities help transform school from a place where we tell students what to think to a place where we help them experience thinking.

Pantomiming, improvising, writing, and acting scenes require fluent, flexible, original, and elaborative ways of thinking. Acting further requires curiosity, taking risks, and imagination. Actors must resolve paradoxes, create analogies, reveal discrepancies, and show change. They must tolerate ambiguity, express themselves intuitively, evaluate situations, and visualize outcomes. In the very act of writing scenes, rehearsing, and performing, drama becomes an excellent tool for exploring, reflecting, experimenting, and assessing.

And in addition to the above, actors learn by preparing a role, researching, getting along with fellow actors, rehearsing, planning, sometimes making sets and costumes, overcoming stage fright, acknowledging the applause, dealing with disasters, and making the show go on.

Decisions, Decisions, Decisions

When we decide what activities work best with our students and we know why, then we are making a difference. To me, this is the heart of being a professional.

From time to time in the Dialogue sections of this book, I'll ask you to make certain decisions about the activities. For example, you might decide to use only specific types of activities; to divide your class in certain ways; to avoid the warm-up exercises; to wait until you feel your students have understood one drama activity before going on to others; or offer them a smorgasbord of dramatic possibilities and let them choose which ones they want to use to show you what they know.

You decide what's best. A kindergarten teacher friend of mine told me she knew that her students had learned some part of a lesson when they repeated it in play. Drama works the same way. My hope is that you'll use the activities as play. Eventually, your students will have a repertoire of dramatic playing skills to draw on when you direct them or when they decide on their own to do group work, make presentations, or perform in more elaborate productions.

Chapter 2

Distributing the Talent

Once you're convinced you want to show your students how drama can help them learn and show what they've learned, the first step is easy. There's absolutely nothing complex about asking your students to begin to act. You're going to ask them to play, but with focus. You will respond to the dramatic activities they already do.

A little information goes a long way. What you gather in half an hour of observation can last you all year. However, you may want to periodically observe them playing as they develop, to present them with greater challenges.

Answering the Dialogue questions on page 16 will help you identify the natural abilities of your students. Your observations and the notes you make will also provide helpful information for placing students in groups so you'll know how to distribute the talent.

You can point out to your students what they already have mastered, but might not have realized. For example, Emily might be confused about what you mean when you ask her to direct a scene about pollination, but she might understand exactly what you mean if your notes show that yesterday she directed other children during free time. She said, "You be the mother, you be the brother, you be the policeman who walks by. No, no go wa-a-a-a-y over there and then walk into the house." A regular Cecil B. deEmily!

DIALOGUE

Which students

• act out more than simple imitations?

_____

_____

• have pretend friends, or love stuffed animals and carry on conversations with them?

_____

_____

• use pantomime in natural play?

_____

_____

• have the best ideas for playing house (or whatever make believe or life-reflective games your students play in your classroom)?

_____

_____

• like to sing?

_____

_____

• like to pretend to fight like the Ninja Turtles, the Power Rangers, the Three Musketeers, Batman, or other characters?

_____

_____

• would like to do any of the above, but don't?

_____

_____

Sharing your Dialogue results with the class will show students that you're paying attention and that their actions, especially in play count. For example, "Julie, when you were a unicorn during recess, I could tell you had a horn because of the way you moved your head."

But most important, observing the successful ways your students pantomime and act will show you the rich abilities they already have to work with. It doesn't matter how well they act; it matters that they do. This fact will help you bridge the gap between their natural play and using that play to develop creative and artistic expression.

Field Notes: Teacher-To-Teacher

I observe how my students interact, how they play, and what they play during their free time. I take a few notes on their physical actions (skipping, running, moving) and how they imitate people, animals, or things. I use a copy of my roll sheet to keep track.

- Julie becomes a unicorn at snack time.

- Rob hears music and begins to move his body in time to it very rhythmically.

- Chuck imitates a bear he saw on a camping trip.

- Josh has older brothers and sisters who teach him the latest dances which he teaches to others.

- Jennifer always plays the mother when the kids play house. She has a way of putting her hands on her hips that makes her seem like she's scolding everyone. It's pretty funny.

- Stephanie imitates whatever Jeremy does.

- Michael can tell you the plot of every movie and television show he's ever seen.

–PGH

I'd like to take a moment to define three terms: *natural expression*, *creative expression*, and *artistic expression*. The goal for the teacher is to work with whatever the students' abilities are at present, and then to enhance these abilities by guiding students through more complex forms of expression. Most students, unless they have been trained at a special acting school, will have lots of natural abilities and little creative or artistic sense. You can help them find their own creative and artistic expressions.

Natural expression includes children's dramatic play. It is highly improvisational, informal, unstructured, and based on prior knowledge.

Creative expression makes the drama important in and of itself. Under your guidance, students will begin to create characters and situations they are learning about. They may consider the character's feelings, thoughts, and emotions. Studying the character's movements, look, and speech will help make their performance more specific than one based on natural expression. Students' performances will be largely for their own education and enjoyment.

Artistic expression adds formal structure and awareness of the audience to creative expression. This type of expression is not self-centered, but keeps in mind what the audience will perceive. Students' performances may be for their own education and enjoyment, but students will also be aware of what educates and interests their audience.

Under your guidance, students will begin to create characters and situations they are learning about.

I suggest that the first "bridge" from natural to creative expression be a simple statement leading from your observations of their play to the first unit of work you want students to understand through drama. You might say something like, "Jennifer, I noticed how you were the mother and got annoyed at your family. The way you shook your finger at your children was funny and reminded me of the way moms really do talk to their kids sometimes. I wonder (now you're edging into a unit on family stories) if you were the mother in that story we read yesterday that took place in colonial times, how would you scold your children? What would you say? What would your worries be?" When Jennifer imagines an answer, then you and she have begun to show the class how acting can work to enhance knowledge.

Over a period of time, repeat this activity with every student. Tie each student's natural abilities to characterizations (real or imaginary, human or not, animate or inanimate) that are connected to current studies in your classroom.

Debrief afterwards by asking each student actor what he or she learned by playing the part; then ask the same questions to the audience.

Once you've built this bridge with your class and they understand that you value their play, they can make the easy transition to projects drawing on their natural expressions. Later you can guide them toward more creative and fuller characters and plots and the deeper thinking that drama brings out in participants. How to do this is the scope of this book.

You're the Director

Directing is pretty easy, but I warn you—and you know this already—it's going to be noisy, a little chaotic, and, as at every first rehearsal in the history of humankind, you may want to give it up. But don't. You'll have to encourage some students, calm others down, and guide everyone because playing in school is a little odd. Did you find a place where it's okay to be noisy? Would your class like to take their shoes off?

The 10-Step Process

These 10 steps provide a secure system for working on all drama activities.

1. Explain to students that they can use drama and acting to help them learn and to show what they have learned.
2. Review the content from the students' resource books, experiments, readings, research, or any other source of knowledge that you want them to translate into drama.
3. Make sure your students know what specific story, action, event, or process they are going to represent.
4. Make sure your students know what roles they are going to play. Actors cannot play a part until they know who the characters are, where they are, what the characters are doing, yearning for, desiring, feeling.
5. Explain the drama activity. The Dialogues in the following chapters will help you create these, and I will offer suggestions to choose from.
6. Set time, space, and touching limits.
7. Ask the class in general or each group to repeat to you the instructions so they know what to do first, second, third, and last.
8. Initiate the activity.
9. Have the students perform the work.
10. Debrief. Ask what the actors learned, and, if relevant, what the audience learned.

The Steps in More Detail

1. **Students use drama to learn and to show what they know.** Each time you engage your students in drama, you should begin by explaining that they're going to use drama to help them learn, understand, and show the whole class what it is they have discovered. Keep bringing the focus back to this, so that students can also focus their work in this direction. When they are concentrating on showing what they know with their acting (as opposed to how many Ninja Turtle fight scenes they can fit into five minutes), then they are working with creative expression.

2. **Students translate content into drama.** Make sure your students understand the concepts and information first. It's okay if they are vague about what they know, as drama can reinforce knowledge or challenge students to learn something in more detail in order to present it.

Drama can reinforce knowledge or challenge students to learn something in more detail in order to present it.

While you don't have to know anything about being a stage director to use drama in your class, you do have to have materials prepared for your students. Student actors need books, encyclopedias, atlases, and, most of all, the words or thoughts of the people they are going to portray. Documents of great help are letters, interviews, journals, and writings by the very people whom the students are studying. But don't worry if you can't get a lot of these materials right off the bat. In three or four years of collecting books and documents, you should have a great primary source library. And a little primary source goes a long way. One or two letters or diary entries will probably suggest as much information as students are likely to need in order to capture a person's voice or to make up their own version of what they think that person may have written, spoken, or thought about.

Even if you decide to use only the books you have available, students can imagine the conversations between people relating to the subject of the book. This shifts the assignment slightly, and it means you will have to teach the students to construct dialogue from their observations. This is often a necessary shift anyway, particularly when there are no documents in the voice of certain people (for example, Zeus, a cave man, or Nefertiti) or when the students are playing nonhuman roles: trees, fluorocarbons, rain, eggplants. Drama specialist Christine Caton offers suggestions about teaching nonhuman dialogue in the Field Note on page 24. I also offer general suggestions about writing dialogue in Chapter 5.

3. **Students create the action or plot.** The point of any scene is that the action in it makes a difference to the people or things involved. If two children meet on the playground one morning before school, and one says "Hi," and the other says "Hi," and then they go off to play with other children, that's not a scene. Nothing changed, nothing happened, it didn't make much difference to anyone. If the same two children met at the same place, but one has brought a fabulous toy that's been advertised on TV for weeks, but only a few are available and he won't share it, you can bet there will be a dramatic scene. Within the scene we would witness acts of persuasion, coaxing, enticement, frustration, obstructing, attempts at convincing, converting, and, maybe if things get desperate enough, selling, bargaining, and even feuding. By the end of the scene, depending on what decisions the characters made, the two characters would have learned a lot about each other's moral, emotional, and physical strengths and weaknesses. Through their words (script) and deeds (actions) they would have come to feel differently about one another.

4. **Students know their roles.** No actors can play characters without knowing something about them. When students begin to create pantomimes, improvisations, or short or long scenes and plays, they will have to learn about the characters, how they sound, what they feel, what they desire, what they say and do, and why they say and do these things. This is why drama is such a handy and authentic way of teaching. When students create characters, they

- put together old and new researched information
- account for discrepancies (Thomas Jefferson both supported democracy and owned slaves)
- find the actual words the characters used or imagine what words the characters said, given the information they have
- put the characters' lives into perspective with their own. For example, there are ways that students declare their independence in normal, everyday life. When acting out a scene about the Declaration of Independence, there are words that will immediately spring to their

minds. After studying the document and the debates that led to the Declaration of Independence, students will come to realize that their words declaring independence sound a lot like those of the framers of the document. But they will also realize in what depth, direction, and manner the framers developed their thoughts. By using their words and the framers' words, student actors playing out a debate will learn how more mature people think, and they'll develop a wider vocabulary to express those thoughts.

For students to create characters from general information, or to play characters who didn't leave a voice print or are inanimate, you have to help them with questions that elicit speech and action.

The question of purpose is one of the most difficult and puzzling questions for students, but it leads you and them to tremendous learning opportunities. What is the purpose of rocks, chameleons, coasts, deserts, or ants? From a human point of view, they have specific purposes; some animals eat other animals and keep the population balanced. But it is an important conundrum to ask the purpose of a coastline, ugly spiders, scorpions, and black mambas. I hope the answers will fascinate your students.

5. **Students understand the drama activity.** Explain the activity simply and concisely. You can start with some of the activities in the next chapters, and also write your own.

6. **Students understand time, space, and touching limits.** Review the time limit with students (which can be extended if everyone is involved and things are going smoothly). Review the definite objective, for example, write the script; choose the roles; research the roles; memorize page one; or run through the whole thing three times without stopping. Review the space limit by telling the students where you want them to work: at their places, in groups, seated on a rug, and so on. Review the touching limit. No one invades another's space with voice, breath, touching, or put-downs.

7. **Students review their next steps.** Depending upon whether this is the first day of the activity or the continuation of an earlier activity, ask each group to review their plans or report their progress to the class. Ask, "What is your next step? What do you need to focus on today?"

8. **Students initiate the activity.** Perhaps this means one or more students work in front of the class audience and you are the guide (Stephanie is a snake losing its skin). It might mean students are working in groups, in which case you are circulating and noting their progress (someone in each group is a snake losing its skin and other students are animals in the environment where that kind of snake lives). Or, finally, you might have all students simultaneously engaged in some activity guided by you (everyone's a snake losing its skin, either at their seat, seated on the floor, or at some other place in the classroom).

9. **Students perform their work.** Create a space to perform the work. Review what good audience manners are. Actors want to please, and it's hard to concentrate on stage if the audience is noisy. An audience is silent unless the activity calls for a good laugh or cry, or interactive response. More importantly, however, there are things a class audience is doing in a proactive sense. They are perceiving and responding and evaluating to what the actors have to share so that when you debrief with the audience, you can count on their responses. Show your students you consider these responses as part of the learning process and build on them.

10. **Students debrief.** Debrief by making sure the audience explains what it learned from the performance and what the performers learned. Use this time for your students to compliment the actors and show their approval appropriately. By appropriately, I mean that an audience member's response contains an example and a "why" that backs it up. For instance, "I liked the way you used a sweater so that it became your skin, because it was interesting and funny to watch," or "I liked the words you used, because they made you sound like someone who lived long ago," or "I liked what the continent of America said to Columbus because that's what I would have said, too."

Further, you might guide audience responses by asking students to focus on actions, characterization, or the process, and what they learned from these. You can also structure debriefing questions to elicit responses about the actors' creative or artistic progress.

Ask questions about what made the performance enjoyable, funny, or made students feel sad, glad, or even confused. The answers would reflect how the performers worked to create these effects.

Field Notes: Teacher-To-Teacher

I use these questions to help students turn nonhuman or inanimate things into actable "characters," using a chameleon as an example.

- What does the character need, desire, or want? (The chameleon needs shelter and food and wants to survive.)

- What can prevent the character from doing or getting what it wants? (Predators prevent the chameleon from living.)

- What can the character do when threatened? (It can change color when in danger.)

- What is the character's environment? (The environment is the forest.)

The next step is to have students turn their answers to these questions into actable moments. I ask the actor playing a chameleon, "How can you show where you are and what your purpose is? What would you say to another animal that prevented you from getting what you wanted? What would you do to prevent being harmed?"

- What is the character's purpose from a human's viewpoint? (Its purpose is to keep the bug population down.)

To give students a sense of their purpose in a scene, have them think of a phrase that uses action to describe what their character wants. For example, when involved in studies about the life cycle, a student lizard might say, "I need to find bugs to eat." A student prey being attacked by a student predator might say, "I need to fight for my life." And, indeed, these are the exact same kinds of statements stage and screen actors pose to themselves to help them create a fuller, more truthful and artistic character.

–Christine Caton

SHOPTALK

Newman, Judith. *The Craft of Children's Writing*. Portsmouth, New Hampshire: Heinemann, 1984.

I mention this book here because no matter what age your students are, they can write plays and scenes. I've seen marvelous performances based on beautiful drawings and writing by early elementary children. Newman's book will be particularly useful to primary teachers and parents. With many examples, she shows how writing reveals a child's growing awareness and use of language in every context. As younger students begin to write their own scenes, this book will help you understand their writing and its connection to the process of learning. Newman shows that learning and development take place on many fronts simultaneously. For this reason, risk-taking and experimentation with written and oral language, obviously benefits the learner. Finally, Newman writes that it is important to have audiences respond to the meaning of what children have written.

Collaborative groupwork gives students more say over their own education, helping them to make more decisions, learn more, and get more stage-acting time.

Grouping Your Cast of Learners

This is an out and out endorsement of collaborative learning while teaching science, social studies, drama, and other subjects. Collaborative learning is perfect for helping students develop creatively on their own and to understand the importance of the arts in their lives. Your job is to show them how to express what they know through drama, visual art, music, and dance. When student groups voluntarily decide to show you what they know about being good neighbors, fighting forest fires, or exploring ancient cultures, then you know that they have fully understood the big picture. With collaborative learning, the translation of information into the visual and performing arts is not overwhelming because everyone helps. Students collaborate best when they know what activities are open to them and what information they are to perform, write about, or pantomime. Groupwork gives students more say over their own education, helping them to make more decisions, learn more, and, obviously, get more stage-acting time. In my one-hour class of 34 acting students, it would take me a week to watch each of them perform a monologue. However, each student can be up on stage two or three times in the week when I ask them to work in groups. This way they also have more to figure out and more to perform; they get more organized and stay focused.

My job is to offer the groups prompts or to debrief with them after I've watched them rehearse.

Field Notes: Teacher-To-Teacher

When you ask students to present what they have learned in an artistic manner (for example, acting out or singing their knowledge about chlorophyll), students get jazzed. But they can also become confused if you are asking them to make a leap that is too abstract or unfamiliar. They may not see the point of turning their careful research into a scene or dance just because the teacher is wild about the arts. They value what they did, and they don't see the point in translating their own work into another form. If at 2:30 someone asked me to pantomime my work day, I'd probably scowl at them and say, "Couldn't I just tell you about it?" After all, I'd just done it! This is why I suggest you give your students the choice of which form to use in presenting their findings. But I also suggest that you help students feel comfortable little by little in exploring art forms to express their intellect. If students have read and learned about a clothes-making machine, one of the things you will help them realize through pantomime is that no matter how cool the sound and movement may be, the action is tedious, repetitive, and noisy—all abstract notions until they experience them through drama. Now the students are ready for insight and empathy when you debrief them with questions such as, "What do you think it would be like to work on that machine in that factory for an hour? a day? a week? What would happen to you if you had to work with the machine for many years?"

—PGH

When you engage students in an interdisciplinary learning experience combining drama with other studies

- you may want individuals to work or perform in front of the class. This is particularly effective if you want each person to show his or her way of acting and learning that takes only a moment to perform.

Example: You've studied how petals open, and each student has studied a specific flower. Now each one takes five to ten seconds to show this movement.

- you may want the whole class to use drama as a learning tool. *Example:* You've studied Columbus's first voyage, and you would like all the students to imagine themselves on the *Santa Maria,* each one taking a different role—officer, sailor, captain. They improvise how they felt being on that leaky tub bobbing around in the middle of nowhere—scared, hungry, cold, and with mutiny in their hearts.

- you may want a specific group to use drama as a learning tool. *Example:* You've studied the machines on which clothes are manufactured; you've shown films about clothing. Now you want to make sure everyone understands the manufacturing process, so the whole class is going to become a factory with each student or group of students becoming (through the magic of pantomime) one of the machines they've studied.

- you may offer the class a choice to use drama as a tool for learning. *Example:* Your class has been studying forests in groups. As part of their work on forests, you ask each group to make a presentation to the class on their finished research. And you offer them the choice of presenting it as a dance, through music, drama, an art project, a newspaper article, or any combination of these. They decide.

Consider these groupings and think about when to make such choices for your students.

From my own experience, I suggest that you

- ask questions if a group doesn't know how to get started or if they stall. Begin again by asking, "What's the task? What do you want to do? How could you do that?"

- ask questions when the students say they are finished with a rehearsal and you think their work is thin or that they need to consider more information. Ninety-nine percent of the time students will be satisfied with what they plan to produce. Ask them, "What is the character thinking? What does the audience need to know?" However, there are times when the students are perfectly happy with their success at their level and my advice is to leave them alone. Note what they've left out and plan to include that information in your next mini-lesson.

S H O P T A L K

Wassermann, Selma. "Children Working in Groups? It Doesn't Work!" *Childhood Education*, Summer 1989.

I learned about group work from Selma Wassermann. She writes that her goal is "to help children move toward greater control over their own learning and themselves...and to invite children to play a major role in the significant decisions of classroom life and learning." Once she informed her students that these were her expectations, she assumed they could take responsibility for their learning. They didn't. She wrote, "It boggles my mind that I would ever have such an expectation. I would never have expected any child to learn to eat with a spoon just because I had presented such an idea...yet I expected of them thoughtful, wise, independent functions." Not only did her students not function in a sophisticated, mature, and self-disciplined way, they begged for a return to "the way we did it in Grade 5." She writes: "The behaviors children exhibit during their first attempts at cooperative, independent group work are likely to be noisy, aggressive, random." Wassermann learned that it takes months for students to become comfortable in the kind of groupings where working together enhances the entire outcome.

Chapter 3

Pantomime

Pantomime is acting without words. It is communicating with gesture or movement and facial expression instead of talking. Pantomime can be as simple as asking your class to participate in a gesture you think will help them understand a concept or help them to show their understanding; for example, pantomiming the leg movement of a frog to understand that animal's muscular system. But pantomime can also be a complete group performance such as Marco Polo's trek from Italy to China. Consider choosing pantomime as an aid to learning or teaching a process, procedure, or system described in your students' books, labs, or observations.

The word "becoming" will help you think of events ripe for pantomime, for example, water becoming polluted; buds becoming flowers; caterpillars becoming butterflies; the continent of America becoming full of railroads; two families becoming friends.

Pantomime is also appropriate when

- the knowledge to be acquired and communicated depends strongly on the five senses (Give students time to explore weight, shape, size, texture, and temperature, allowing their senses to be developed and to make the pantomime more believable.)
- you are teaching students with special needs, students who don't speak much English, shy students, and students whose motor development is more advanced than their oral skills

- the action or props to be pantomimed are in reality prohibitively expensive (a nice-sized emerald), rare (a moon rock), unavailable (a woven basket made from reeds), or hazardous (toxic waste).

Before you or your students have selected what you want to learn through pantomime, do some warm-ups. Students can do them individually at their seats, in a sitting circle, or standing. You will have more control if your students are seated to begin with, and they will not lose out on most of the activities. Review the rules about touching.

- Pantomime is not a contact sport.
- Honor other students' personal space.
- Do not invade another student's space with your breath, voice, or body unless given specific directions (as when you ask your class to pantomime the interlocking parts of a working machine).

Coaching

You will need to coach your students from the get go. I urge you to allow the students to work out their own actions. Although you might coach a lot from the side and offer encouragement, try to keep your direction of their movements to a minimum. If they seem lost, remind students of facts they might use and the conclusions the class came to, but allow them to create their own movements. Don't, for example, move a student's arm until it looks the way you think a pantomimed tree branch should look. Your student may feel perfectly like a tree and may be understanding all kinds of things about root structure, photosynthesis, and leaf design but is not ready yet for artistic expression (that means, in this case, pleasing you—the audience member). Although in some cases, you might ask individuals to move more exactly, or to move only an identified part of the body. Don't worry, artistic expression will come to students after they have understood what it means to pantomime a tree.

If you've set groups of students to work on their own, and you see that the children are engaged in an activity, encourage them to explore it from angles they may not have considered ("Your flying reminds me of a delicate butterfly. How about showing how it felt to break free from your cocoon?").

When students' work seems vague, ask them questions about the details—weight, shape, size, texture, and temperature—to help them make the imaginary look real. For example, "As you lift that bale of cotton onto your shoulders, can you show how heavy and bulky it is? how hot you are?" Or, "As an Athapascan Indian, what does your fur robe feel like?"

To make pantomiming comprehensible to your students, I suggest you start with the warm-ups and practice suggestions that follow. When your students understand them, move into your curriculum. You can insert your curriculum at any point, and I have offered many examples of doing this throughout the warm-up exercises. On the other hand, if your students are already doing pantomime, skip to "Pantomiming the Learning Event" on page 34.

Field Notes: Teacher-To-Teacher

At any time, you can introduce material from the social studies or science learning event you are studying by asking the students to pantomime movement or react to something emotional. For example, if you are studying deserts and their ecology, ask the students to walk as if through a desert.

—PGH

Pantomime Warm-ups and Practice

- Students move their heads in circles, then add their hips, knees, and finally toes, until the whole body is going in circles.

- Students move their head in a jerky way, then add their shoulders, arms, and legs until their whole bodies are jerking. You can vary this with other movements you like: mechanical, clumsy, rubbery, oiled, gushing, happy, silly, or wind-blown.

- Students move across the room or stay in place showing slow motion as if walking, climbing, running, or skipping—through jello, mud, or quicksand. They move as if blindfolded and feeling their way, as if lifting a heavy weight with each part of the body, or as if balancing on a tight rope.

```
DIALOGUE

Consider using pantomime as one of the modes of learning in
your current science or social studies learning events.

What important processes, procedures, changes, or adaptations
do I want students to focus on?

_____

_____

Of those I listed, how would pantomime help students better
understand?

_____

_____

Write a pantomiming prompt that would focus your students on
understanding. Remember to include the word "becoming."

_____ becoming _____

What research will the students have to do to gather enough
information to perform the "becoming?"

_____

_____

What warm-ups, if any, will I do? _____

_____

How will I group the students? _____

_____
```

Pantomiming with Natural Expressions

After these warm-ups, you can begin to show students that a lot of their natural expression is pantomiming. Ask them to show how they move their arms if they know the answer to a question and really want you to call on them, how they move their mouths if they want something delicious to eat, how they breathe if they've just run a long distance. And there are countless other ways we all pantomime, like showing how our feet feel if they've walked a long time, how we flick water off our hands, or how we would pick up something icky, hot, sticky, soft, delicate, dangerous, or light. If your class can do all these, then ask them to combine them. For example, show picking up something hot and sticky, running barefoot over muddy ground or warm sand, or flicking a dangerous spider off their fingers. If you can, make references to the information you gathered in your Dialogue in the last chapter, noting how you saw certain students doing this already, and how exact they were. Use this information for examples and encouragement.

Pantomiming with natural facial expressions. Ask the students to kneel and rest their chins on the flat surface of the top of their desks or tables. Now ask them to show silent reactions to the following descriptions. They can move only their face and head.

- They are watching a scary movie.
- They are eating popcorn and the kernels get caught between their teeth.
- They see something funny, but aren't allowed to smile or laugh.
- They're watching a race and their friend comes in first or comes in last.

Facial expressions are equally important when students play non-human character roles. Ask students to react to the following situations, again using only their faces and heads to convince an audience of who or what they are.

- They are a pasture and a crop duster just dropped insecticide on them.
- They are parched soil and it begins to rain.
- They are a desert and travelers on camels are walking on top of them.

Picking up invisible objects and moving them. Brainstorm with students what objects they might encounter in the learning event you are studying. Select one and think about it in terms of weight, shape, size, texture, and temperature. Now they are ready for you to teach them about picking up invisible objects.

Field Notes: Teacher-To-Teacher

I use these six easy steps to make the imaginary look real. Explain to your students that they are going to learn to pantomime handling and using imaginary objects by practicing with a cup. Have the students set an imaginary cup down in front of them and then perform the following activities:

1. **Look.** With the object resting on the floor, table, or sink, look at it.

2. **Reach.** Move your arms, hands, body in the direction of the object to show your intent to touch or pick it up.

3. **Grab.** Grasp the object in an appropriate manner (hold the cup the way you naturally do with both hands, or a couple of fingers and your pinkie up).

4. **Use.** Handle the object in a natural way (for example, drink or sip from the cup). Show how you feel about the object—the drink in the cup might be cold, sour, hot, or sweet.

5. **Stop using.** Stop the action and place the object at rest either at the same place where you picked it up or a new place. Don't bring it to rest in mid-air!

6. **Release.** Take your hands away from the object. Make sure you don't set the object down and then move your hands through or over it because when you pantomime this action, it will look like you are knocking over the object.

–Christine Caton

Pantomiming the Learning Event

If your students are successful in their pantomime warm-ups and practice, you're ready to move into the learning event you want them to explore. Decide if you want students to work in groups or individually, soloing in front of the class, or working alone, with the understanding that later on each student will show his or her work to the entire class. You might give your students permission to move around if you feel they can do so without becoming disruptive, but a lot of action can take place at one's seat.

Give the prompt when you are sure students have enough information to do the action. When you debrief, help students understand they can isolate certain natural actions to create an impression. For example, imagine you are teaching a lesson on problem solving and one student is pantomiming how another snatched her ball away. After she has shared her pantomime, you might ask her if she would like to isolate a particularly important part of her piece. She might isolate the snatching motion, her reaction, or the reaction of the student who took her ball. Alternately, you could ask her to isolate certain moments for the class to learn from. Ask them to talk about how the ball was snatched and what they saw in her pantomime. Then cut to the chase and discuss what students learned from the action. Was it harder than they thought? Did it use muscles they don't normally use? Did it remind them of other actions? What's something new that they understand about a person (animal, thing) that does that action?

Field Notes: Teacher-To-Teacher

You can add some nice touches. Students in your class might learn about how birds eat by picking up a peanut from a clean desktop using only their mouths. To shed their skins, student snakes may have to inch out of a blanket or, if they want a real challenge, a loose-fitting sweater that their arms aren't in while lying on a rug and keeping their hands in their pants pockets. If you assign students to work on this pantomime at home, they have the opportunity to bring in their own props (one of my students brought the sweater I just mentioned). Their ingenuity will amuse you, and, moreover, their ingenuity is a sign that they are moving their acting from natural expression into creative and artistic expression.

—PGH

Pantomimes of inanimate stationary objects help students understand the structure of things.

Suggestions for Group Pantomiming

Each member of the class becomes a part of a machine in movement with another part of the machine. The activity begins with the movement of one student who, for example, might raise and lower his arm as if pounding in a nail with his fist. Another student stands next to the first student so that the first student's fist taps her shoulder. When she feels the tap, she makes a quarter turn to the left and sticks out her foot. A third student enters the "machine," and, when the second student sticks out her foot, this taps the third student, who bends over. A fourth student enters and when student three's forehead touches his finger, student four wiggles his finger in the air. Continue adding one student at a time until eventually the whole class is involved. Students may need your guidance and suggestions to help them coordinate their timing with people behind and in front of them.

When the class can do this imaginary machine, they are ready for real machines and processes. If you have studied how bakeries make bread, then students can pantomime that process. Pantomime can be used for showing any process, movement, or "becoming"—for example, cars at stop signs and stop lights; actions of peoples of other cultures making or doing something; people playing instruments; the Boston Tea Party; what happens to garbage; how timber is turned into lumber; how one group of people migrated to another part of the world; the nesting activities of bees; flying formations of swallows; the movement of cloud types; the fall of raindrops; medieval war machines (like catapults); train pistons; and steam engines. The actions can be as complex or as simple as you wish.

Pantomimes can also represent inanimate stationary objects that aren't becoming anything. Students can pantomime different parts of a shelter or parts of cathedrals (stained glass windows, flying buttresses, gargoyles, arches,

domes, aisles, apsis). This helps students understand the structure of things, and why things are built or constructed the way they are. As always, the more the students have researched and studied the things they are pantomiming, the more successful the pantomime.

Pantomiming in pairs. You might want to use these warm-ups before you ask pairs of students to pantomime newly researched information. Two students help each other put on roller skates, ice skates, or any other kind of athletic equipment. Two people help each other make a campfire, feed an animal, or build a sand castle. Two people can pantomime playing tennis, checkers, or other sports. (Avoid boxing and wrestling, but sword fighting is fine if their invisible swords are very long!) Best of all, students can be pairs of things in the curriculum like sun and rain helping plants grow; animals with symbiotic relationships; pairs of people in history (the Wright brothers, Lewis and Clark); pairs of people who work together (doctors and nurses, singer and guitarist, the one who pulls the plow and the one who sows the seed).

Bigger pantomime projects. You may want to have the whole class tell big stories, showing the natural processes of historical events or daily actions. The advantage to this is that you often don't have to worry much about a script if you've read a wonderful biography, poem, or journal entry. Someone reads it during rehearsals, and the students perform it. For a performance, you may or may not choose to have someone read the text depending on how clear the pantomiming is and how comfortable the students are about performing without directions. Finally, you can add music (taped or the children's own) to that polished theatrical spectacle which your class work has now become.

You may want to use scripts to help actors remember what to do. Scripts are pieces of writing and drawing. Scripts can be

- children's first attempts at writing in which they use whatever letters, diagrams, and drawings they can
- highly polished documents that constitute one piece in a complete portfolio of a student's work
- a collaborative effort that you and your students write, or one that they write in groups.

The scripts might begin as student reflections about what they saw being pantomimed, or journal entries that carefully reconstruct the day's activity.

Whether you make your pantomimes formal or informal is based on the decisions you have made about your students' abilities, what would best help them to learn, and the direction you want to take the assignments.

Using Pantomime To Spark Thinking

Students use pantomimes to make predictions. If your class has completed only half an experiment on water pollution, students can pantomime what they predict will be the outcome. Using pantomimes to make predictions can be particularly useful when studying something that involves movement such as cell division, how water finds its level, or the migration of early peoples. In these instances, have students feel their surroundings, examine the limits, the texture, the temperature, and the strength of the area, then predict and pantomime the best way to move. You and the class may want to discuss the possibilities thoroughly before trying them out. The pantomime might help the class decide which options seem reasonable and why.

Pantomimes that lead to "What if…" situations. Imagine two students are rehearsing cell division and they start getting silly and making up lots of cells and mutant cells. This gives you the opportunity to ask, "What if our bodies go haywire and cells start splitting into sixteen parts?" Such a question will lead students to further research. You can also throw in a glitch to create a "What if…" situation. For example, if your students are showing you their pantomime on the migration across the Bering Strait, you can throw a wrench into the proceedings by asking them to imagine and pantomime what would happen to the group if someone became ill. Your debriefing will lead to all kinds of interesting conclusions and moral dilemmas. You can "tune" the scenes by suddenly changing the weather and land conditions, and emotional situations. You can introduce situations you observed in the classroom that morning that prevented good learning or hurt someone's feelings. Finally, you can suggest silly or exaggerated conditions as did the students working on cells.

Pantomiming a world contrary to the facts. What would have happened if the Wright brothers' plane never got off the ground? What if your ancestors hadn't come to this country? What if the ocean stopped making waves, fish could fly, snakes had feet, or our knees were on the back sides of our legs?

These suggestions will direct students toward creating original solutions, finding patterns and relating them to what they understand, transforming information, and engaging in divergent operations.

Students create original solutions, finding patterns and relating them to what they understand.

Moving from Natural to Creative and Artistic Expression

When students move through the continuum from natural to creative expression and into artistic expression, their work begins to change in two general ways. The performers begin to perceive their characters as their own creations and, as such, value them. Also, the drama becomes important in and of itself, meaning that performers can see their drama activities as a process by which they come to know and understand. Secondly, as students move into more artistic expression of their work, they become more aware of their audience and make acting choices that help the audience better understand what the student actors have learned.

Creative and artistic expression are the aesthetic building blocks that help students to learn and to express their learning.

Field Notes: Teacher-To-Teacher

My speech students were concerned about a proliferation of intolerance in our community. They decided to bring a drama activity to a neighboring elementary school and chose the fifth grade to work with. My students wrote scenes in which people were confronted with situations in which intolerance, prejudice, and injustice seemed a possible outcome. Each scene depicted a poor choice that led to confrontation or misunderstanding. They performed the scenes for small groups of fifth graders and, after, asked a fifth grader to step in and perform the scene in such a way to successfully avoid violence, intolerance, or disrespect. Clearly, while my students had weeks to write and rehearse, the elementary students had only a few moments to think, respond, and then to act. And they were not used to drama in their curriculum. On the other hand, my students would repeat their lines and actions as often as the elementary students wanted, and would wait until the children had thought of a solution before they went on.

Because of how focused my students' scenes were, and because the story structure was clear, the fifth graders quickly dropped their natural acting (vague lines, silly responses, silence) and began to explore possible outcomes (creative expression). After one or two runthroughs, some elementary students performed their scenes with my students for larger groups of fifth graders who received them enthusiastically. In debriefing, it was clear that the fifth-grade actors had not only communicated what they learned to their peers, but to my students as well. They had learned how to analyze difficult situations and respond to confrontation.

–PGH

Creative and artistic expression are the aesthetic building blocks the students are acquiring and developing that help them to learn and to express their learning. These building blocks are in every way as valuable as the comprehension or computational building blocks students need in order to become better readers and mathematicians. And just as your students are always building with these cognitive blocks, sometimes making mistakes and sometimes surging ahead, so too will their pantomimes reflect creative exploration and an understanding of audience. Sometimes their work will seem unfocused to themselves or to an audience. Their creative and artistic expressions may last a few moments or become a complete performance of an hour or more. It is important to discuss in debriefing how the students use artistic and creative expression, how they use drama as a tool for learning, and how they make what they learn clear to an audience.

As I mentioned earlier, the goal for the teacher is to work with whatever abilities students have at present, and then to enhance these abilities by guiding them through more complex forms of drama. Begin by discussing with students any natural pantomiming you've watched them do. Perhaps it was dancing, or laying an invisible blanket over a sleeping doll, or wielding an invisible weapon. Once you have focused your students' attention on these activities, showed them they are valuable, and encouraged them to perform activities like these in your classroom, students  will begin to realize that their natural actions can lead them into knowing and learning.

Students might not naturally begin to use drama to explore new sensations, ideas, or processes. To encourage students to explore more and more of the creative and artistic continuum, your job will be coaching or guiding from the side while students are using pantomime to learn. Here are some coaching questions and strategies.

Coaching to evoke creative responses. Keep asking the students to show, show, show. Show what that feels like, show what that tastes like, smells like, sounds like. Show what you feel. Show how hard that is, or how easy, how much, how many, how often. The best questions will be ones that you have thought about before the activity that will guide students to learn the subject matter through action. You can explore these same questions during debriefing after the activity.

DIALOGUE

Are my students ready to pantomime what they are learning on their own in collaborative learning groups? If so, how will I help them write their own "becoming" prompts?

_____

_____

_____

How can I plan activities that will help students working in groups?

_____

_____

_____

What kind of coaching statements will I make?

_____

_____

_____

What coaching questions can I or the class ask that will spark thoughtful analysis?

_____

_____

_____

What debriefing questions can I anticipate asking that will help students add to their knowledge? (For example, if they have all been snakes losing their skins, then one debriefing question might be, "What happens to the skins after the snakes have abandoned them?")

_____

_____

_____

_____

If you see that students are having trouble showing an action clearly, then focus their attention on the part of the body they need to make more exact. For example, "Show what your fingers do when you hold that glass. Show how your toes dig in to give you traction as you climb up that sand hill. Show what your mouth (eyes, cheeks, nose) looks like when you're chewing something you don't think tastes very good."

Coaching to evoke thoughtful analysis. Guide your students by asking them to explore a movement, activity, process, or feeling—following up on a previous pantomime. For example, "Yesterday you were wonderful as butterflies coming out of your cocoons. Today as you do this activity, show what you have to do with your wings, what your wings feel like, or what flying for the first time is like."

Another suggestion is to ask students what questions they have about what they are studying before they pantomime. Then ask students as they pantomime to use their actions to explore the answers. You might ask them to explore one answer or to brainstorm many. For example, if you are studying people-to-people problem solving, some students might have questions about what to do if they are eating at a friend's house and don't like the food. Students using pantomime can explore many different answers. During the process of pantomiming and in debriefing, the students can figure out which solutions are reasonable or appropriate.

Students realize that their natural actions can lead them into knowing and learning.

Coaching to evoke predominately artistic responses. Help students think about what the audience is seeing as they perform their pantomime. Could someone else see what you are holding? Could someone else tell what you are doing? Could someone else know how you feel or how you fix a thing, hammer it, or cut it? Could someone else tell how to do that for him- or herself?

Debriefing. By coaching and rehearsing, your students will become more and more convincing. You will know this when you debrief and students say they could literally "see" the invisible objects, and the characters seem genuinely engaged in the action. Students in an audience might say, for example, "Cara looked like a butterfly climbing out of a cocoon," or "Jeremy and Domenic really seemed like two people using their own sign language to communicate the ideas of welcome and friendship."

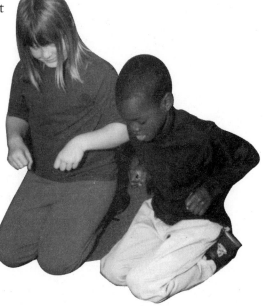

When you ask your students to invent ways to demonstrate their work, you are instilling in them an additional direction toward more creative work. For example, the student who brought in a sweater to help show the snake shedding its skin found an elegant and artistic solution, one everyone understood, enjoyed, and wanted to try. Why? Because it was an artistic solution which meant that it was pleasing or interesting to look at and taught the class something new—what it might feel like to be a snake losing its skin. The best solutions are always ones the students themselves dream up.

Chapter 4

Improvisation

As I walked into Cheryl Nelson's primary classroom in Mary Farmar Elementary School in Benicia, California, some of the children were making cards for their parents and others had the choice of listening to "The Nutcracker" or "Chicken Soup with Rice" on a tape recorder. A few of these children couldn't decide which story to listen to and began hitting each other. Two of the combatants got up and told Nelson about their fight. Nelson finished helping a student glue his picture to a card, and then she gathered the class onto the rug in the center of the room.

She asked the boy who had been most outraged to tell what happened. Then she solicited a few more versions of the scenario from children who had been in the listening corner and finally a version of the events from children who had just been watching. She asked some of the students to reenact the event, but without the hitting. They did so, each of the two students involved saying one or two lines apiece. Then she asked other students to reenact the event, and she solicited from them and the class some ideas for more successful outcomes than a fight. The class quickly decided the characters could offer to listen to first one tape and then the other. The boy who had been the most frustrated played his part with passion and accuracy both times. By the time he finished acting the second scene, he was satisfied he had learned a simple, new, and peaceful way of handling the event. Then everyone went out to recess.

Nelson is excellent at letting students do plays and act out their lives and the stories they have read. But she is also very careful not to allow the activities to get out of hand. One way she keeps some order, she says, is that she herself often plays the person the students would perceive as mean or bad, while other students play themselves. She is also careful to explain to the students that acting is not real, so they are not to get out of hand throwing punches when they are Ninja Turtles or jumping on each other when they are cowboys riding off on their horses.

Field Notes: Teacher-To-Teacher

I went to Mary Farmar Elementary School in Benicia, California, to visit Cheryl Nelson's primary class of six and seven year olds. In the past, I have worked with Nelson by bringing my drama students to her classroom where my students help hers produce plays. The younger students would try out different stories and scenes one way, and then another. Sometimes the Ninja Turtles flew on the backs of tenth graders; sometimes the eleventh graders became mountains on which the beautiful unicorn princess sat. They tried out a lot of different movements and possible twists of plot until everyone was content with the scope of their pieces. Then we acted them out. When I think of improvisation, I always think of Cheryl Nelson and her class.

–PGH

Here are some of the qualities Nelson's improvisation had:

- It was immediately important to her students.
- It was short.
- It did not require a script.
- It could be acted by different people.
- It had definite and identifiable characters.
- It had a definite, real, and understandable conflict.
- It taught the students who performed and who watched something more than they knew before. It gave them a lesson in their own words and actions.

Getting Started with Natural Expression

An improvisation is an unrehearsed moment "on stage." The actors have a lot of researched information on which to base their improvisation, but the fun is they don't have to practice before they perform. It is pretty easy when students play themselves. With enough information, students can learn to perform characters based on their science and social studies thematic learning events by improvising. An improvisation can last five seconds or much longer.

I would suggest that to introduce your students to improvisation you follow Nelson's process. Begin the students' introduction to improvisation by asking them to reenact events from your classroom. Too close to home? Then ask them to reenact events that have bothered them on the playground this week. Some students might enjoy improvising events that had happy outcomes such as when others included them in a game or when others complimented them. An improvisation might take a second: the reenactment of a funny noise, a silly giggle, a fire engine that went by with sirens blaring. An improvisation might take longer if a student isn't focused on the moment he or she wants to show. You can be of help by asking a student to focus on the one activity of recess he or she would like to show the class.

```
DIALOGUE

Consider your experiences with your present class. What
moment would you like the class to examine through a reen-
actment improvisation? Or you could have students choose
their own reenactment moment. In either case, think of an
example with a happy outcome and one with an uncomfort-
able outcome.

_____

_____

_____

_____

If one of the characters in the event is perceived as threatening
or a cry-baby, who might take the role other than students?

_____

_____

_____

_____
```

If you begin improvisations based on the students' own school lives, they will understand the process after a couple of sessions and be able to see how their improvisational abilities help them learn and show what they have learned. My hope is that if your students have begun to improvise moments of their class lives, they will make an easy connection when you suggest that they use improvisation to interpret their lessons about families, pollution, or an event in American or ancient history.

Your first forays into improvisation may require a lot of prior discussion, side coaching, and eliciting lines and gestures from other class members. Your students will improvise more fluidly as they become comfortable with the skill.

D I A L O G U E

Here are other questions to think about when planning student reenactments:

What might my students say for the dialogue? (Usually one or two lines for each character is all that's needed.)

_____

_____

_____

What could I say as coach to help students develop the dialogue and test other outcomes?

_____

_____

_____

What grouping would work best for this activity?

_____

_____

_____

What questions or prompts could I pose to my class during debriefing? (Don't forget to ask the actors and the audience what each character desired.)

_____

_____

_____

_____

_____

Improvisation with Science and Social Studies

1. First complete steps 1–4 in the 10-step process described in Chapter 2.
   - Explain to students that they will use improvisation to learn and show what they know.
   - Review the information with your class about the people or things they will act out. It's very helpful if students can examine the original words of the people they are studying.
   - Discuss with your class the conflicts and tensions the characters had or are likely to encounter.
   - Assign very specific roles and make sure the actors understand the desires of their characters.

2. Introduce your students to new elements in acting, learning, and performing that are necessary for creative expression.

   Remember, all actable moments involve tension. You can create scenes of tension when you tell your cast to persuade, coax, entice, frustrate, obstruct, convince, convert, bargain, or feud. Desire is the character's reaction to tension, and it is the most important thing that actors attempt to make clear to audiences. In fact, all acting may be said to boil down to making desires clear to the audience through words and actions. For example, during a learning event on pre-revolutionary America, ask your students to improvise a scene between the royalists and the colonists in which the royalists frustrate the colonists with higher taxes. The royalists' desires are clear, and their desires are going to create in the colonists some pretty concrete and actable desires of their own.

   Ask students to tell you what their characters desire. "I want to   (verb). I want to congratulate him. I want to stop her. I want to explore that continent. I want to hear her footsteps. I want to help her climb a tree." So, now that your students know what they will improvise and who they are, ask them what they think their characters will desire in the scene. They can't go on stage until they tell you. If they're having trouble, you can coach them and get audience suggestions.

3. Whereas students can pantomime individually and in fixed places, improvisations are initially done by small groups of two or more in front of a class. You will need a small acting space and an audience that understands it will be learning and participating. Later on, when students master some of the craft of improvisation, they can work in groups to develop more sophisticated scenes as discussed in the next chapter. For now, the improvisations will require your assistance and coaching.

4. Assure the actors that this is not instant improvisation. They get to talk it over for a while before they act. Your students have done this before when they engage in natural expression and improvise the life around them, cartoon characters, or special events that interest them. At first, they'll need you to help them apply these techniques to the improvisation exercise. To this end, give your students time to plan. Guide them by helping them to decide where actors will be placed at the beginning of the scene, what the action will consist of—in a general sense, who does what, who says what, and who desires what. You might help them establish a clear protagonist (hero), antagonist (villain), or simply two clearly conflicting forces. The more certain your students are of their characters, their desires, and what they are trying to show, the more focused their improvisation will sound, the more relaxed they'll be, and the more likely they will be able to use improvisation as a tool for learning.

Field Notes: Teacher-To-Teacher

A little word of warning. On a natural level, improvisation may seem uninspiring to you, but it isn't for the students. Their first attempts might just be an introduction of who they are. (I am an eggplant, I grow on vines, I like lots of water and sunshine. I am a watermelon, I grow on vines, I like lots of water and sunshine. Do you see a pattern emerging?)

Eventually, improvisation can be pretty interesting when students play people or things and have had experience saying what comes to their minds about who or what they are. The most elegant example of this type of creative or artistic expression might be a student who has become absorbed in a character such as Sojourner Truth, reads a lot about her, and as a final project, entertains the class with anecdotes from the person's life, selections of the person's letters, odd thoughts, funny events, memories, and opinions.

Cheryl Nelson
Mary Farmar Elementary School
Benicia, California

5. Assure the actors that they can end the piece in any number of ways and that one way is not better than another. Also assure the actors that it is a perfectly normal part of the creative process to become

stuck, stymied, frustrated, or run out of ideas during an improvisation. It takes a lot of practice to improvise. It's like letting everyone see the intimate ways your brain works before you've had a chance to refine your thoughts and make them presentable—the way you want them to be seen. It is important that the audience understands this, too, at the outset, so that rather than viewing students who are tongue-tied in front of the class as a couple of dolts, the class responds to them in a friendly manner—everyone understands that this is a process. Just because people aren't talking doesn't mean they aren't thinking. So, first tries may not work well but the improvisation is a very important part of the process of critical thinking and of art.

6. Now it's time to go for it. Initiate the activity by asking the actors to perform for the class and make up what comes to their minds based on the information the class has learned or discovered about a subject. Review the situation as much as is needed, side coach, ask for suggestions, and assure the actors they can stop when they've clearly run out of material. (For purposes of explanation, let's assume the improvisation is about the Declaration of Independence. Before, during, or after your study of the document, you ask some of the class to improvise a discussion between those who supported the ideas in the Declaration and those who were royalists.)

7. In debriefing, your class should reflect on what they learned. Be on the alert for questions the improvisation raises about the material. From the Declaration example, some questions might be: "What would happen if the royalists were more convincing in your class improvisation than the framers of the Declaration? How could the framers have dealt with threats to life and limb? What emotions did the royalists have and why? What issues did everyone seem caught up in and why?"

The big reward will occur later when students will recall what they said in improvisation and find out to what extent they predicted well and what new information they have gathered.

The big reward for this improvisation will occur later when, having studied the document and the events leading to its creation, students will recall what they said in improvisation and find out to what extent they predicted well and what new information they have gathered.

DIALOGUE

In the learning event your students are studying now or are about to study, what action, process, or event would lend itself to improvisation? Look for these kinds of relationships: predators and prey; people, animals, or objects with opposite viewpoints or desires; people or things that need each other to survive; animals, people, or things that camouflage or adapt themselves for protection; the tempter and the tempted; the aggressor and the victim; paradoxes or the unexpected; and opposites such as hot and cold, storm and calm, big and little.

_____

_____

_____

Who would the characters be? And what would each character desire?

_____

_____

_____

What factors (problems) might I introduce to help students analyze, synthesize, and judge?

_____

_____

_____

What coaching do I think my students might need?

_____

_____

_____

_____

When To Use Improvisations

To demonstrate what has been learned so far. A good use of improvisation is to demonstrate what's been learned by the whole class so far. Simple improvisations can repeat what students have read in a book or seen in a film while the actions and words are fresh in their minds.

To nurture critical analysis. Suppose you want to work on critical thinking. Stop a film, a reading, or research halfway through, and ask your class for improvisations that predict outcomes. Make sure you follow the seven how-to steps on the prior pages, especially number 4 so that students have specific information and know the things all actors need: who they are, where they are, exactly what action or impulse they are to react to. Here are some examples:

Improvisation A: Your class has read about Columbus sailing west and about his crew's hostility, but they haven't read about him reaching land. Several students are Columbus, his crew members, officers, sailors. How does Columbus convince them to go on?

Improvisation B: Your class has seen a film about the construction of the pyramids in Egypt; but before you show the part that explains how those enormous stones were lifted into place by people who had no electrical cranes, motors, or engines, ask the class to improvise how they might have lifted the stones into place.

Improvisation C: Your class has studied immigrant families leaving their homelands and coming to America. Improvise what might happen when immigrant children follow their parents' traditions in this country or what might happen when they follow American ways.

If you manipulate the improvisations midstream or at the beginning, if you throw in an unexpected problem, more information, or even remove certain factors, then you can challenge your students to learn to deal with ambiguity, paradox, practical and ethical problems, and account for discrepancies. No matter what you do, however, the actors have to be certain of two things: exactly who they are and what their desire is.

Here are some critical thinking factors you can play with:

- Switch the environment, particularly if you want students to predict outcomes or to understand and apply a concept they have already learned to a new situation. For example, if you have studied the geographical areas Lewis and Clark explored, ask two students to be the explorers and set the scene in the eastern area of what is now the state of Washington. How would they start a campfire? How would they start a campfire if it were raining? If the class

You can challenge your students to learn to deal with ambiguity, paradox, practical and ethical problems, and account for discrepancies.

has studied the colonies in early America, ask them what effect the environment had on the course of history—how it affected the daily lives of people who didn't have air conditioning, plumbing, or central gas heating. You might ask students to improvise a conversation at a town planning meeting in the event of a great harvest, and then ask the students to replay the scene assuming there had been no rain, or a terrible winter in which half the population was wiped out.

- Switch characters if you want the students to deal with emotional empathy. For example, a student sees someone in the playground with a toy she would like to play with. In an improvisation, the first student asks the other if she could play with the toy. Now ask the first student to imagine the other student is a stranger, then a best friend.

- Switch atmospheric conditions to help students predict action. Your class has studied seeds, roots, stems, and plants; and now one student is a plant that has grown up in a nice moist, rich soil with plenty of sun and rain to grow. What does that look like? What would the rain, soil, and seed talk about? What if there's no rain and the sun beats down? What would the conversation be between the sun, plant, and soil?

To demonstrate learning at the close of a learning event. By its spontaneous and fluid nature, improvisation lends itself well to the beginning and middle of learning events, particularly when trying out or predicting effects, consequences, and outcomes. But here are some ways to use improvisations at the close of research, too:

- Improvisation can work like the game charades. After completing a study, the class makes up a set of cards, each one containing an event, process, or procedure from the study. A group draws a card and improvises the scene written on the card.

- A group of students improvises a scene from commonly shared studies, but they do not mention any names. The audience has to guess who the various characters are by what they do and say, where they are, and how they interact.

- Students pick characters they would like to play from the same study, and they improvise an event that could have taken place between these characters. In life, perhaps these people never met, and your students will have to make up their own story. For example, in studying about the environment, your students read articles about people who affected environmental changes in their communities. Some of these people may have lived long ago, some may be living next door to the school. Others may be living in other countries. The improvisation asks students to assume the roles of these real people and to have a conversation. They might try to solve a social, political, or ecological problem.

- Students improvise sounds, first deciding on culture, region or area, and make sounds that would be heard there. The audience has to guess where the area is. Or, hand out cards to each group of students who then work together to plan and perform the sounds. Here, as elsewhere, consider how well pantomime can be combined with acting.

```
┌─────────────────────────────────────────────────────────┐
│                     DIALOGUE                              │
│                                                           │
│  What might my students learn through an improvisation    │
│  that they might not learn as well another way?          │
│                                                           │
│  _____      │
│                                                           │
│  _____      │
│                                                           │
│  In what ways would it work best to group my students?    │
│                                                           │
│  _____      │
│                                                           │
│  _____      │
│                                                           │
│  What circumstances can I change that will lead to        │
│  rethinking and replaying the improvisations?             │
│                                                           │
│  _____      │
└─────────────────────────────────────────────────────────┘
```

Coaching. Here are some specific suggestions about coaching for more creative and artistic improvisation when you see that students have lost their concentration or do not know what to do next. You could use these suggestions during the improvisation itself to guide students' learning, or during a debriefing.

- Coaching statements and questions that evoke predominately creative responses: "What does your character desire? Tell more about _____. Explore that idea, emotion, thought. How would you react to that? What clues does your environment give you for action? What solutions might come to this character? What might he, she, or it try?"
- Coaching statements and questions that evoke predominately artistic responses: "What are the character traits or desires that the audience has to understand most of all? What additional information needs to be acted out so the audience understands? What information have you studied that you might include in your scene?"

I'm sure anyone who's taught for even three minutes understands that the life lessons learned in classrooms are as vital and as permanent as the lessons about phonics, science, or math. But just as academic lessons have to be reinforced, so do thoughts about getting along, inclusion, respect, and many other life lessons. Drama is an excellent way to reinforce positive attitudes. Drama strongly reinforces the attitudes and lessons you work hard to help your students understand. Remember Nelson's students who fought over which story to listen to? They found a solution, with the help of their classmates, through improvisation. Nelson's children were not perfect angels on the playground when they went out to recess that day, nor did anyone expect them to be. Yet Nelson had set an important example for her class: in her classroom, if you get angry, you can find solutions, resolutions, and solace for your problems.

SHOPTALK

Scher, Anna and Charles Verrall. *Another 100+ Ideas for Drama*. Portsmouth, New Hampshire: Heinemann, 1987.

Excellent practical advice about running improvisations—what to do when an idea falls flat on its face, how to prepare yourself for all kinds of eventualities. The examples are geared toward the daily life and experiences of students, and provide opportunities (especially for younger children) to use characters as positive but believable role models. Direction, Professionalism, and Criticism are some chapter titles. Chapter 5, on full-scale productions, contains practical information about audiences, voice projection, mistakes, concentration, quiet, and consideration.

Wassermann, Selma. *Serious Players in the Primary Classroom: Empowering Children Through Active Learning Experiences*. New York: Teacher's College Press, 1990.

Wassermann suggests some of these prompts. She uses them in debriefing, but they seem appropriate for helping tongue-tied students, too. "What observations did you make? How did you know that? How did you figure that out? Tell me about what happened. What parts of the event did you like? What parts were funny or sad? What was hard for you to do or say? What was easy for you to do or say? How could you explain that to another person whom you like? What problems might occur if you said or did that? And finally, and very important, what did you want to happen? What did you desire?"

Chapter 5
Writing and Acting Scenes

A scene, in most classroom contexts, is a codified improvisation containing the opening to a story, its middle, and a definite end. Scenes can take a minute to play, or longer; they can be sewn together with other scenes to form a play. Shakespeare's *Hamlet* has twenty scenes that together run four hours or more. How long your scenes last is up to you and the students, but the form or structure is the same.

In first-draft form, students progress from the natural form of improvisation to creative and artistic scene expression through two vehicles, the *script* and the *rehearsal*.

Writing, editing, and polishing a script helps students organize their knowledge. Rehearsing the script and then reworking it based on what students discover in rehearsal helps them plan how to present their knowledge to the audience. This process helps students think about what it means to amuse, impress, and teach others. As they consider the audience's reaction to their creative work, their expression moves to an artistic level.

Since scene writing requires someone to write and some people to act and revise, I suggest a group-oriented model through which the work can be completed.

DIALOGUE

Scripts help you and students assess student learning. To help your students turn their pantomimes and improvisations into scenes, first think about their skills and how they communicate.

How do my students write? Can they formulate their ideas on paper in a clear way? Can they write quickly?

_____

_____

What's the easiest way for students to write down what they and others improvise? Would a tape recorder help?

_____

_____

Like improvisations, you can use scenes before a learning event, during it, or at the close to help students make predictions, analyze, judge, and synthesize.

There are a couple of places to begin scriptwriting with your class. You might begin by observing that the class or study groups are having a lot of fun or success with improvisation or pantomime. They are able to show some interesting information about what they learned. Because their improvisations are going well, you might offer them the chance to codify their work. So their first scenes might be improvisations written down. The group recorder might do the writing, or a parent, you, or an aide. The written scene might be a series of diagrams, pictures, and words.

The second level of scene work asks students to consider their improvisations, enlarge them, choose what worked in them, discard what didn't, and prepare a scene script from many improvisations and discussions.

The last level is for students to write a play from scratch, using all the knowledge of the unit they are studying.

SHOPTALK

Sklar, Daniel Judah. *Playmaking: Children Writing and Performing Their Own Plays.* New York: Teachers and Writers Collaborative, 1991.

Use everything you can from this book. Sklar's approach to creating an animal, object, natural (wind, sun) or human character is simple and direct. He has students answer certain questions in character and then write about their performances. His questions and "Character Profile" writing assignments focus the actors and help them to use acting and writing to learn and to create believable moments on stage. Some of the character backgrounds he asks students to consider while playing roles are name, age, family, wishes, fears, and habitats.

This is the best book on teaching drama in an elementary classroom I have read. Sklar narrates how he taught a drama unit in which students wrote and produced their own scenes dealing with themes of importance in their lives. In each chapter, Sklar writes about the concrete problems students naturally run into when they don't understand the purpose of drama or feel their voice is not heard. His examples, debates, decisions, and doubts are real because he voices our own dilemmas and writes about them eloquently.

Scene Structure

As students begin to write their scenes, help them understand ideas of structure. The following examples will give them a form they can follow to translate their text information, learning, experiments, and so on into a scene.

1. Balance—The characters show their relationships to each other at the beginning of the scene. Characters can be angry, content, oblivious, and so on.

   The three little pigs are living happily.

2. Disturbance—A character or event disturbs the balance, forcing the main character called the protagonist to make a decision, to take action.

   A wolf disturbs their happiness by trying to eat the three pigs. One pig makes a decision to destroy the wolf.

3. Rebalance or resolution—The action of the protagonist leads to a solution of the problem.

The smart little pigs trick the wolf and return to their happy life.

In Shakespeare's *Romeo and Juliet*

1. The Montagues and the Capulets are feuding.
2. Romeo Montague and Juliet Capulet fall in love and decide to run away so that they can be together. Due to miscommunication, they both die.
3. Their deaths convince the Montagues and the Capulets not to feud and these two noble families promise peace in their town.

In Dickens' *A Christmas Carol*

1. Scrooge is miserly, and Bob Cratchet, his clerk, is poor and starving.
2. Scrooge is shown the errors of his ways in the past, present, and future.
3. Scrooge decides to reform and becomes generous; bestows food and money on the needy; and Tiny Tim, Cratchet's sickly son, does not die.

Balance

The first task of your actors is to establish what the balance is, in other words, to show the way things are right now before anything is disturbed. Younger children can show this by telling you at the opening of a scene, "This is our block and these are the neighbors." Older students can achieve this through conversation. For example, two three-hundred-year-old giant redwoods open a scene talking about their lives. Balance usually helps to establish characteristics: who is hot-headed, who is cool, who is a fussbudget, who is kind, who is mean, who is searching for something— love, treasure, food. You can suggest to your students that balance sets the stage, establishes the characters, and lets the audience know where they are.

Years ago playwrights used to have servant characters or underlings (often comic) open the play describing the events their masters were involved in. It was often funny and full of gossip. At the opening to Mozart's opera *Don Giovanni,* for example, Leporello, Don Giovanni's servant, sings about how his master charms women, whereas he, Leporello, has to take the heat and look out for Don Giovanni's skin. Writers also introduced their plays this way because audiences were notorious for walking in late, and this was a handy way to entertain, set the stage, and keep the audience warmed up until everyone was seated. About ten minutes into the play, the major actors would step onto stage and get the plot rolling.

In your class, help the students set the balance in a few moments. Gossip, as above, is a good way, or try these opening lines:

Have you heard about_____?

Did you know that _____?

What do you think about _____?

Can you believe what happened?

Hey, what are you doing? (or any other challenging lines)

Here are some examples of balanced situations:

- Two bears hibernating. It's spring and time to wake up. One wakes up, nudges the other, and says, "What do you think about getting up? We've been sleeping for two months straight!"

- Two Native Americans speaking about some strangers they have heard about. The year is 1550. "Did you hear about that tribe near where the Mohicans live?" says one. The other replies, "I don't believe everything I hear." The first says, "They say the strangers' skin is white like the inside of potatoes. And they have a stick which, when they point it at you, kills you."

- A river and a river bank. It's spring. The river tells the bank it's going to burst any moment. It can't hold back. The bank begs the river not to. "Look at all the life that will be destroyed." But the river says, "It's bound to happen. I can't control myself."

Once the balance is established, and reveals the news of what's to come, it's time to write the main part of the play.

The Disturbance

In this part, more and more difficulties are piled at the feet of the main character, the protagonist. These difficulties are centered around

- the protagonist's own personal qualities that stir up trouble (his or her greed, laziness, haughtiness, or other weakness). It's best if the protagonist is not a bad person, but one with a flaw that gets him or her into hot water.

- others' arguments, personalities, desires, or emotions.

- physical or natural impediments or obstacles (landslides, a swarm of piranha).

When the difficulties become overwhelming, the protagonist has to make a decision right then and there, in front of the audience. We see the character decide what to do. Will he or she be successful?

- Here is where we see the two bears actually confronting their spring world. What if there's been a terrible forest fire (a physical or natural impediment) while they slept? Finally the main bear has to decide what to do, how to gather food (they're very hungry), or how to migrate. The bear character decides to migrate. Is this the best choice?

- Here's where we see the two Native Americans confront the Europeans. What if the Europeans are lost, terrified, and dying of starvation? The main Native American has to decide what to do, how to help the Europeans, or how to destroy them, or a million possibilities in between. The character decides to ignore all the bad things he or she has heard and help the Europeans. Was this wise?

- Here's where we see what life will be destroyed by the rising river and how farmland might be lost. The main characters may be insects that have burrowed in the ground or the plants who have to decide what they can do. Some have no choices. Which can survive being covered by water? Which have other adaptive means? What will people do about the rising river? Will humans or insects survive better? The insects decide to swarm away. What will become of them?

Rebalance or Resolution

This part of the play shows the result of the protagonist's decision to act, and ends the action.

- Because the two bears have decided to set off in search of better forests and trust their sense of instinct and smell, they avoid hunters and end up in another part of the forest.

- Because the Native Americans decide to help the Europeans, they trade some of their food for blankets. Neither party realizes, however, that the blankets contain germs that carry diseases.
- Because so much silt is deposited by the raging river, the insects made a good choice. The lands are, in fact, unfarmable for many years, and the riverbanks have to support different kinds of life.

One last word about balance, disturbance, and rebalance or resolution—the structure is not an exact science. Some students may argue that certain action takes place in the disturbance and others might say that same action should be part of the rebalance or resolution. It doesn't matter, as long as the action is complete and makes sense.

D I A L O G U E

In an upcoming science or social studies learning event, what events or processes have a definite balance, disturbance, and rebalance or resolution?

_____

_____

What educational benefits are there to writing and performing scenes?

_____

_____

Am I willing not to grade first drafts on spelling and grammar and save mechanical considerations for the final draft?

Organizing Students Into Groups

You will have to consider class organization for writing, rehearsing, and producing scenes. If you would like to make group work part of scene writing or if you have students already grouped, then I suggest the following which is based loosely on Selma Wassermann's *Serious Players in the Primary Classroom* (1990). I'm going to describe three models for group projects, from simplest to most complex. As always, you are the best judge of what works in your classroom.

Model 1. A student writes the play. In early elementary grades, this might look like drawings and eventually a few words. The playwright chooses people from the class to act out the parts while he or she reads the script. Alternately someone else might read the script, particularly if the writer wants to play one of the really juicy roles.

Model 2. If you, a parent, or older student can come in to help, or if your students are a little older, their scripts can eventually omit the narrator and cut right to dialogue which the actors have to rehearse and memorize.

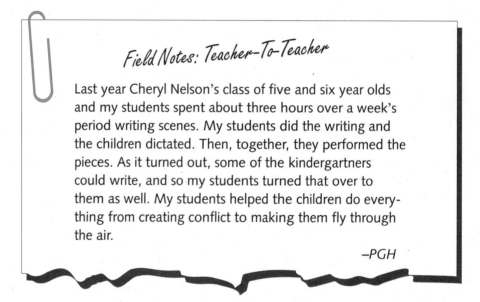

Field Notes: Teacher-To-Teacher

Last year Cheryl Nelson's class of five and six year olds and my students spent about three hours over a week's period writing scenes. My students did the writing and the children dictated. Then, together, they performed the pieces. As it turned out, some of the kindergartners could write, and so my students turned that over to them as well. My students helped the children do everything from creating conflict to making them fly through the air.

—PGH

Model 3. The group decides on, or is given a theme, focus, or assignment. It might be very general; for example, show what you've learned about geography or sea life. It might be more specific; for example, show what you've learned about the symbiotic relationship between two animals, or show the effects of oil spills on herring.

Each member of the group has a duty. The *agenda keeper* makes sure everyone stays on task by pursuing answers to questions.

- What is the subject of the scene?
- What will the balance, disturbance, and rebalance or resolution each be about?
- Who will take which part?

The *scriptwriter* writes down the others' ideas, lines, and actions. The student might want to use a tape recorder or ask an older student to help. Everyone will contribute to the ideas in the script and use improvisation to create the words and movements.

Note: It might not be practical for one person to write down what a bunch of improvising actors are saying and doing, but eventually the agenda keeper calls for order and the piece is codified by the scriptwriter. The finished script can be machine copied or each student can hand copy the whole thing.

The *harmonizer* encourages, expresses group feelings, and suggests compromise. In the case of two people wanting the same role, the harmonizer might suggest that the part can be double cast and then both people, one after the other, can perform the part.

The *stage manager* gathers props and costumes.

The *director* might have no acting role in the play itself or a small one. The director watches the rehearsals and makes sure everyone knows the words of the script, helps people memorize, and makes sure that during rehearsal the actors face the audience.

D I A L O G U E

Can the students work productively in groups if each student has a specific task? How can I get some older students or parents involved in overseeing some of the groups and train them to ask good prompting questions?

_____

_____

Do my students have enough sources (journals, letters, literature) about the characters they are going to portray? If not, or if the characters are inanimate or nonhuman, what materials do I need to give my students so that they can imagine what the characters might say and do?

_____

_____

How long do I think the scene should last

_____

How will I assess students' work?

_____

_____

Which of my students would use pantomime, improvisation, or scene work if I gave them free choice to present what they knew?

_____

How To Use Scenes with Science and Social Studies

1. Complete steps 1–4 in the 10-step process described in Chapter 2, page 19.

   - Explain to your students how they will use drama as a vehicle for learning and showing what they know.
   - Review the information with your class about the people or things they will act out. It's very helpful if students can examine the original words of the people they are studying through primary sources such as letters, speeches, and journal entries.
   - Discuss the conflicts and tensions the characters had or are likely to encounter.
   - Remind the students about character desire.

2. Form learning groups each containing at least five members who assume the roles described on pages 66 and 67. If groups contain more students, then I strongly recommend that you assign other roles for the other members based on what might be needed for your class (safety monitor, costume maker). Explain group assignments.

S H O P T A L K

Cohen, Elizabeth G. *Designing Groupwork: Strategies for the Heterogeneous Classroom.* New York: Teachers College Press, 1986.

In *Designing Groupwork*, Elizabeth Cohen suggests excellent ways to choose students for group learning. There are so many factors in designing groups and materials for them that I like to have Cohen's book available on my desk particularly when I am ready to plan or when students aren't getting along, or are not performing as I would expect. Cohen's book is excellent for re-explaining "it" to me at the end of a weary day or week. She is encouraging and extremely practical.

---

3. Be a coach. When students have completed a draft of a script and are beginning to rehearse it, watch them and offer suggestions. First of all, they have to understand that the script is fluid, and they can change it. You might also use the following method I adapted from Selma Wassermann's *Serious Players in the Primary Classroom* (1990):

   - Ask the students to perform what they have prepared.

WRITING AND ACTING SCENES   69

- Debrief by commenting on what you liked very specifically. For example, "Jennifer, I liked your crabby tone of voice when you said you didn't want to get out of bed."
- If some aspect of the rehearsal seems vague to you, ask students to tell you about that moment. Elicit from them their purpose, and then tell them what you saw. Then ask the group for suggestions about how to make their work more exact. Are there facts they could draw on? If they were in a similar situation, what would they do? What are the problems facing the characters? Have students include their responses to these questions in the script.
- If you see some basic production problems, again frame your remarks as questions. "Eric, I noticed when you were acting with Chuck that you kept looking down. I wonder why you did that?"

4. Help students write the final script. For students who are just learning to write, their own symbols and spellings are fine. For students who can write out the dialogue, I recommend the formats in "Guilding Your Lily: More Stuff To Do for a Production" on page 71 but as always, their own creations are more valuable than my suggestions.

If the students are building on what they've learned and have written the script, they will know what to do during rehearsals.

5. Give the students lots of time to rehearse and rewrite, rehearse and rewrite, improvise, rehearse, rewrite. When the editing is over, then the students rehearse the final product. The point of these rehearsals is to allow students to take a scripted work and practice it enough times so that the characters and events are clear and obvious to the audience. This development of artistic expression will make the audience attentive and will give the performers a sense that what they did was worthy of the audience's support and respect.

Rehearsal time need not be long, but you do need to have the students focused on their work. Usually, if the students are building on what they've learned and have written the script, they will know what to do during rehearsals.

A focused rehearsal makes things easier. Here are three ways to help students focus:

- Memorization—Can the students get through the piece with their lines and actions memorized?
- Meaning—Can the students infuse their lines with meaning? This requires good coaching and stopping the rehearsal to ask, "How do you feel or think about what you are saying or doing?

How can you show with your body or voice what you feel or think?"

- Voice loudness—Can everyone hear the actors?

Have a talk with the audience before the presentation about helping the actors out by not talking as this can impair their focus.

Field Notes: Teacher-To-Teacher

Here are a couple of important tips to help the rehearsal process become a little smoother. I've adapted some suggestions from Elizabeth Cohen's Designing Groupwork (1986).

1. Delegate authority. Each student has a primary responsibility in the group: writing the script, making up characters, planning a setting, directing the action, making or getting the materials with which to construct a set or background.

2. Nip in the bud behaviors that are counterproductive. Label them and discuss them openly in an objective way. Ask in what way they hindered. And then give the group a chance to practice the new behavior.

3. Ask your students to follow these norms for collaborative learning:
   - say your own ideas
   - listen to others
   - give everyone a chance to talk
   - give reasons for your ideas and discuss many different ideas.

—PGH

6. Perform the scenes. A performance is a repetition of the very last rehearsal. The theory is that the group or class is so familiar with the activity that no matter how nervous people may be, they can project their characters to the audience.

If your class is going to perform before a larger group, talk together about how natural it is for everyone to be frightened at performing before an audience for the first time. You can reassure your students that being nervous isn't a bad thing. Lead them to also understand that the audience wants them to succeed, that the audience wants to be amused, and that they (your students) are very amusing.

Actors need to get into character before they perform. This might take from 30 minutes to a couple of hours. Here is a quick way to focus your cast. A minute before they are to perform, ask them to stand in the place they are going to begin from. Some might be "on stage," some off. Ask them to think hard about what their character desires.

7. Debrief.

S H O P T A L K

Sloyer, Shirlee. *Readers Theater: Story Dramatization in the Classroom.* Urbana, Illinois: National Council of Teachers of English, 1982.

While the thrust of this book is to show how to adapt fiction into plays, the adaptation methods outlined are useful when translating your research material into scenes. Sloyer shows you how to take narrative or exposition (writing that isn't dialogue) and transform it into conversation. In chapters about classroom procedures and production aids, Sloyer offers practical strategies and techniques about adapting work in your classroom. The second half of the book depicts a model Readers Theater Program in an elementary school: easy-to-follow, day-by-day, step-by-step games, improvisations, production solutions, vocal exercises, and small-group rehearsal strategies.

Guilding Your Lily: More Stuff To Do for a Production

This is a format for script writing. It works well because it makes everything very clear.

- Describe the setting and each character on the first page.
- On the next page, the first page of the script, describe the action that begins the scene: "Two men are talking," or "Two people run in, one chasing the other."
- Whenever there is action, put it in parentheses before a character speaks.

- Name each character before he or she speaks by centering the character's name in the middle of the page.

Below is an example of the first and second page of a script.

The Setting:
A seashore on a West Indian island.

The Cast
Columbus: Happy to have landed, but wondering what he can find of value.

The First Mate: Thinks of mutiny.

Sailor: Just grateful to touch land again.

Native American Chief: Puzzled by Columbus and the ships, and is very cautious.

An important man in the tribe: Wants to welcome Columbus with open arms. He sees the arrival as a great sign.

An important woman in the tribe: More cautious than the chief, she wants nothing to do with Columbus or his men.

(Columbus and his men row to shore in a long boat.
When they get to shore, they wade to land and
speak to the men and women gathered there.)

Columbus:
I claim this land in the name of Queen Isabella and King Ferdinand of Spain.

Native American Chief:
What kind of language is that?

Native American Man:
(Walking to Columbus to welcome him.)
Let us show these people they are welcome here.

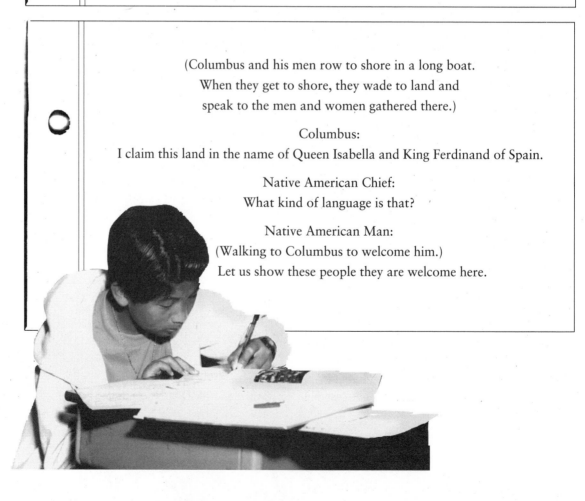

Coaching from Creative to Artistic Expression

Here are some specific suggestions about coaching for more creative and artistic scene writing. You might use these questions while students are writing their scenes, at the end of an improvisation, or as suggestions for improvement while a scene is being tried out. To evoke predominately creative responses, ask the following questions:

- What does your character desire to do? Tell more about _____. Explore that idea, emotion, thought.
- How would you react to that?
- What clues does your environment give you for action?
- What solutions might come to this character?
- What might he, she, or it try?
- What journals or stories have you studied, or can you research, that might help you to give the characters a voice?

To evoke predominately artistic responses, ask the following questions:

- What are the character traits or desires that the audience has to understand most of all?
- What information can you include that the audience might need in order to understand your scene?
- What information have you studied that you might include in your scene?
- What sets, costumes, or props will help this production get the information across?
- Where should actors be positioned—stand, sit, kneel—during the scene?

You can add music and song to any piece. While it is not in the scope of this book to suggest how to teach music or singing, I suggest the following:

- If your class knows or can learn some songs that would enhance a production, go for it.
- You might want to have the students take standard songs they know, and write different words to them which pertain to the action of their scenes.
- You could use instrumental music for plays. The international music section of your local record store will probably have music that would go nicely as background to any period or culture you are studying. Play the music nice and loud to introduce the piece and maybe at the end, but turn it off or play it very, very quietly in the background during the speaking parts and coach the students that they will have to talk loudly over the music.

- Students can, if they want, make their own instruments and play a score they have written to punctuate dramatic moments. To do this, students first make their instruments out of bottles, dried squash, key rings, or other materials. Then they experiment with them and find out the range of possible sounds they can make. A student composer-conductor can create a piece by pointing to the instrumentalists he or she wants to hear at a specific time. Students can write out the score using graphs and symbols. I recommend using music especially if the music is integral to the culture or era students are learning about.

Have you had some successes this year? Would you like to feature your students' work on a larger scale and go into "show business?"

S H O P T A L K

Page, Nick. *Music as a Way of Knowing*. Strategies for Teaching and Learning Professional Library, The Galef Institute. York, Maine: Stenhouse Publishers, 1995.

There is a wealth of knowledge for all educators in *Music as a Way of Knowing*. Page explains how making and sharing music is educationally sound and then offers techniques for bringing music into the classroom and across the curriculum. He shows how the rhythm of music aids our learning, how singing builds community, and how music adds to the joy of living.

Chapter 6

The Big Production

If by now you want to go the whole nine yards and have your students perform their pantomimes, improvisations, and scenes for a larger audience, then you may want to incorporate masks, makeup, costumes, sets, and lighting into the production. In professional settings, these elements are carefully thought out and relate to the psychological moments of the drama. In the case of student theater, masks and makeup help the audience see and understand the actors. If you feel your students can be understood and easily seen in the performance area without makeup or lighting, then you probably don't need these elements. But if you feel students playing bears, for example, really need bear masks or makeup and special lighting, then there are many ways to do this inexpensively to add to the learning experience.

I have to confess right off the bat that I have little experience with the arts and crafts of theater, nor is it in the scope of this book to give you detailed guidelines for mask, scene, and costume making. However, let me say that creating these can be an extremely important part of students' learning. Making masks that resemble bear faces or caves that resemble real bear caves require student research as educationally valid as any other method of learning.

Some aspects of theater work such as nailing sets together or stringing lights teach construction, muscular coordination, getting along, and working together—all valuable learning. Your consideration, however, should be, "Do I want to teach all these ancillary skills? Do I have the time? the energy? Could I get someone else to do it?"

If you have a community theater company in your town or a junior college or even a high school with a drama department, then a polite call to them for sets, costumes, and lights (and a person to run them) is not out of order.

There are lots of books that can show you how to make sets, sew costumes, and put on makeup so that a ten year old looks ninety. The thrust of this book, however, is to help you and your students learn collaboratively. By this I mean the children should make as many decisions about their scenes as possible. If a child who is to play the part of a bear has designed bear claws out of popsicle sticks, a bear mask using a brown paper bag with a few brown circles drawn with crayons, and found a brown overcoat in the school lost and found, and put that all together to make a bear outfit, I say that's great. Think of all the decisions needed to create such an assemblage! If his parents sew or get him a bear costume, is the actor much better off? For most students I've worked with, their own ingenuity in creating costumes and props is part of the fun of learning. In a student-centered curriculum, I would hope the students would be deeply involved in making their own masks and costumes.

Students' own ingenuity in creating costumes and props is part of the fun of learning.

If you have a box of remnants or old clothes, that's all you really need.

The Stage

If your school has a stage, consider using it, but there are lots of other places where you can put on your plays. Your room might be easier to transform into a set than the stage. Or, perhaps there is a small stage at another school that has more facilities. You could also use a small gym with bleachers. Another idea is to use a multi-purpose room with enough large and sturdy tables to create a safe stage.

Masks

The Greeks used masks to help expand the sound of the actor's voice. They were enormous things with megaphone-type mouth pieces. I don't recommend these for your students, but I do recommend that for whatever masks you make, make sure the eyes and mouth are not covered in any way. An effective way to achieve this is to create Zorro-type eye masks. These can be decorated in any way, and can also be added to by gluing on paper or light cardboard to the top, sides, or bottom. In this way, you can enlarge their shape and carefully avoid the mouth. Inexpensive Halloween masks are useful too, because you can cut away the mouth and chin parts completely and decorate them as desired. Let the children's hair come over the top of the mask and hide the edge or edges. Children can also make a character mask to hold in front of them. Children affix popsicle sticks to a face mask they draw and paste a matching outline to the back. Voilà—they've created their own characters.

Children have an innate sense of what can make them seem like the character they are to play.

Makeup
The primary concern with makeup is that it does not harm the students' skin. If you, a parent, or other adult knows how to apply theatrical makeup, this might be a possibility for creating characters, particularly very old or very odd-looking people or things.

Costumes
I think that children have an innate sense of what can make them seem like the character they are to play. If you have a box of old clothes, or pieces and remnants, then the children can create their own costumes.

In context of the kind of education I am suggesting, I think it best that children make their own costumes their way. If this is impractical, then deciding with parents what kinds of costumes can be constructed from the children's own wardrobe will probably work. For example, a child can wear a scarf to look like a pirate.

Sets
If you produce the plays in your classroom, then the tables, chairs, and children's art are the sets. Students can learn a lot from planning how to place these pieces in such a way as to offer a suggestion of the setting. Again, their planning and learning to rearrange objects to create an effect is of much greater educational value than buying or making them a realistic set.

If you need special set pieces, then the easiest way to make them is with large cardboard facades taped to desks or chairs and then decorated to look like a cave, time-travel machine, ocean, or the setting of your choice.

You can create a mood by projecting a slide onto a white background. The picture will disappear once you have turned on other lights, but if you keep the lights off and the slide projector on for about 10 seconds before the students start to act, then you can "suggest" the setting and the audience will assume you are there until you show them another slide or tell them otherwise.

You can also create interesting effects if the actors are wearing white and move in front of the slide. If you can get some clear film and let the children color on it, and run it as a loop through a 16mm projector, then you will have beautiful moving patterns that you can project onto white backgrounds or white costumes.

Since I have little talent constructing realistic sets, I have had to rely on other things to suggest scenery and sense of place and atmosphere. The best thing I've come across is PVC pipe which is very cheap—about 55 cents for ten feet. It's pretty safe for all students to use (though they need to be careful of the rough ends after you've cut them). If you teach upper elementary school students, they can easily saw the pipe themselves under supervision. You and the class can put the pipes together like Legos with connecting right angles and other joints. You can create cheap, big, sets that students themselves can move. The sets won't support any student's weight—they can't walk or swing on them—but this piping is great for making frames and is solid enough for you to hang fabric on. You can also make outlines of buildings or interesting geometric shapes.

Another advantage of PVC is that you and your students can design the set together easily. Almost anything they can draw with a straight edge can be constructed by them if you have enough of the right connecting pieces. When you have the set the way you like it, you can use duct tape to keep it together. For ten or twenty dollars you can make all the sets you want from PVC, and you can also stack it easily after the show.

SHOPTALK

Miller, James Hull. *Self-Supporting Scenery: For Children's Theatre...and Grown-ups' too. A Scenic Workbook for the Open Stage.* Colorado Springs, Colorado: Meriwether Publishing, 1982.

From trees to houses to lamps to thrones, Miller's book helps you construct free-standing sets that don't have to be hung from ceiling rafters or pipes, or bolted to the floor. Miller's examples can be adapted to be used with everything small- or large-scale, from cardboard boxes to theater scrims and flats. While the book covers specialized hand tools and offers complex construction advice, a teacher who wants to make a particular set piece will be able to use the diagrams and instructions.

Lighting

If you are performing on a true stage, then lighting becomes something of a problem. Stages are dark places and their box-like shape tends to suck up light. If your stage or stage area comes with adequate lighting, then you are in luck; otherwise you might find some of the students are performing in darkness or shadows. The best way around this is to rent one or two theatrical lights from theatrical lighting supply houses and bolt them to weighted poles (moveable volleyball net poles work very well because they are weighted). Be sure to secure the cords so nobody trips on them.

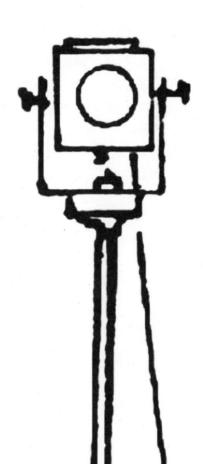

You can create great special effects with flashlights, and you can add colored cellophane over the tops. I do not recommend candles no matter how pretty they are, nor do I recommend anything else involving flames or fire (lamps, lanterns). These instruments are probably not allowed in your school.

Organization

When I do a major production, I ask all the parents of my students to help. There are a variety of committees they can serve on: makeup, costumes, set building, refreshments, and supervision. One parent is head of each committee, and this usually entails about two or three hours of work for each person for the whole production. If you have a student-centered curriculum, then the parents might come into the classroom and help the students make what they need from costumes to cookies.

Supervision is very important. The supervisor's job is to look after the students who are not immediately rehearsing in your classroom or on stage. This will give you the opportunity to give your acting students your full attention.

I'd like to end here with your students giving you their full attention. If you've come this far, then congratulations! It is perfectly all right for you to lay down the law now, to insist stridently on lines being memorized, to fulminate at chaos, and blow your whistle for silence. You are, after all, producing nothing short of a masterpiece and you only have a few days or weeks to make sure everything goes right when the curtain goes up. You have carefully guided and encouraged your students to think well on their own, to show you that they know their way. You have encouraged them to try new things, to learn from their mistakes, and they have genuinely amused and delighted you. And you have shown them how to show you, themselves, and the world the range of their knowledge and thinking.

So take a bow, and break a leg.

Professional Bibliography

Bedard, Roger L. "Challenges to the Field: Working Together," *Design for Arts in Education,* November-December 1989.

Bridges, Lois. *Assessment: Continuous Learning.* Strategies for Teaching and Learning Professional Library, The Galef Institute. York, Maine: Stenhouse Publishers, 1995.

————. *Creating Your Classroom Community.* Strategies for Teaching and Learning Professional Library, The Galef Institute. York, Maine: Stenhouse Publishers, 1995.

Brown, Victoria. "Drama as an Integral Part of the Early Childhood Curriculum," *Design for Arts in Education,* July-August 1990.

Bruce-Crim, Marna. "Writing in the Content Areas," *Instructor,* February 1992.

California State Department of Education. *Prelude to Performance Assessment in the Arts.* Sacramento: California State Department of Education, 1993.

Cohen, Elizabeth G. *Designing Groupwork: Strategies for the Heterogeneous Classroom.* New York: Teachers College Press, 1986.

Dakos, Kalli. "Oh, the Stories I Could Tell!" *Instructor,* November-December 1991.

Durland, Frances Caldwell. *Creative Dramatics for Children: A Practical Manual for Teachers and Leaders.* Kent, Ohio: Kent State University Press, 1975.

Everson, Barbara J. "Considering the Possibilities with Improvisation," *English Journal,* November 1993.

Farris, Pamela J. "To Be or Not To Be: What Students Think About Drama," *The Clearing House,* March-April 1993.

Gardner, Howard. *Frames of Mind: The Theory of Multiple Intelligences.* New York: Basic Books, 1983.

Gehring, Sandra. "It's Not Just Science—It's Life: Teaching Science Through Gardening," *Instructor,* March 1993.

Geoghegan, Wendy. "Re-placing the Arts in Education," *Phi Delta Kappan,* February 1994.

Hansel, Nancy H. *Evaluating Children's Development in Creativity and Creative Drama.* San Francisco: R & E Research Associates, 1977.

Heathcote, Dorothy. *Collected Writings on Education and Drama.* London: Hutchinson, 1984.

Heinig, Ruth Beall. *Improvisation with Favorite Tales: Integrating Drama into the Reading/Writing Classroom.* Portsmouth, New Hampshire: Heinemann, 1992.

Johnson, Terry and Daphene Louis. *Bringing It All Together. A Program For Literacy.* Portsmouth, New Hampshire: Heinemann, 1990.

Klutz Press editors. *Face Painting.* Palo Alto, California: Klutz Press, 1990.

Laughlin, Mildred. *Social Studies Readers Theater for Children: Scripts and Social Development.* Englewood, Colorado: Teacher Ideas Press, 1991.

McKerrow, Margaret. "The Public Image of K-12 Theater Education: Can It Change for the Better?" *Design for Arts in Education,* January-February 1988.

Mda, Zakes. *When People Play People: Development Communication Through Theater.* Atlantic Highlands, New Jersey: Zed Books, 1993.

Miller, Etta, Bill Vanderhoof, Henry J. Patterson and Luther B. Clegg. "Integrating Drama into the Social Studies Class," *The Clearing House,* September 1989.

Miller, James Hull. *Self-Supporting Scenery: For Children's Theatre...and Grown-ups' too—A Scenic Workbook for the Open Stage.* Colorado Springs, Colorado: Meriwether Publishing, 1982.

Morgenbesser, Martin. "Teaching as Improvisational Theater," *The Whole Language Catalog,* edited by Kenneth S. Goodman, Lois Bridges Bird and Yetta M. Goodman. New York: SRA: Macmillan/McGraw-Hill, 1991.

Nevarz, Sandra, Raquel Mireles and Norma Ramirez. *Experiences with Literature: A Thematic Whole Language Model of the K-3 Bilingual Classroom.* New York: Addison-Wesley, 1990.

Newman, Judith. *The Craft of Children's Writing.* Portsmouth, New Hampshire: Heinemann, 1984.

Oaks, Harold R. "Performance vs Content in Theater Education," *Design for Arts in Education,* May-June 1988.

Ohanian, Susan. *Math as a Way of Knowing.* Strategies for Teaching and Learning Professional Library, The Galef Institute. York, Maine: Stenhouse Publishers, 1995.

Page, Nick. *Music as a Way of Knowing.* Strategies for Teaching and Learning Professional Library, The Galef Institute. York, Maine: Stenhouse Publishers, 1995.

Parry, Christopher. *English Through Drama: A Way of Teaching.* Cambridge, England: University Press, 1972.

Pearson-Davis, Susan. "Drama in the Curriculum for Troubled Young People: Is It Worth the Fight?" *Design for Arts in Education,* November-December 1988.

Pinciotti, Patricia. "Creative Drama and Young Children: The Dramatic Learning Connection," *Arts Education Policy Review,* July-August 1993.

Rycik, Mary Taylor. "A Playwriting Primer," *Instructor,* April 1990.

Salazar, Laura Gardner. "Assessment in Theater Education," *Design for Arts in Education,* May-June 1992.

Scher, Anna and Charles Verrall. *Another 100+ Ideas for Drama.* Portsmouth, New Hampshire: Heinemann, 1987.

Schon, Donald. *The Reflective Practitioner.* New York: Basic Books, 1983.

Sklar, Daniel Judah. *Playmaking: Children Writing and Performing Their Own Plays.* New York: Teachers and Writers Collaborative, 1991.

Sloyer, Shirlee. *Readers Theater: Story Dramatization in the Classroom.* Urbana, Illinois: National Council of Teachers of English, 1982.

Turner, Thomas N. *Stand Up and Cheer!* Glenview, Illinois: Scott Foresman, 1990.

Wassermann, Selma. "Children Working in Groups? It Doesn't Work!" *Childhood Education,* Summer 1989.

_____. *Serious Players in the Primary Classroom: Empowering Children Through Active Learning Experiences.* New York: Teacher's College Press, 1990.

Watts, Irene N. *Just a Minute: Ten Short Plays and Activities for Your Classroom: With Rehearsal Strategies To Accompany Multicultural Stories from Around the World.* Portsmouth, New Hampshire: Heinemann, 1990.

Professional Associations and Publications

The American Alliance for Health, Physical Education,
Recreation, and Dance (AAHPERD)
Journal of Physical Education, Recreation, and Dance
1900 Association Drive
Reston, Virginia 22091

American Alliance for Theater and Education (AATE)
AATE Newsletter
c/o Arizona State University Theater Department
Box 873411
Tempe, Arizona 85287

American Association for the Advancement of Science (AAAS)
Science Magazine
1333 H Street NW
Washington, DC 20005

American Association of Colleges for Teacher Education (AACTE)
AACTE Briefs
1 DuPont Circle NW, Suite 610
Washington, DC 20036

American Association of School Administrators (AASA)
The School Administrator
1801 North Moore Street
Arlington, Virginia 22209

Association for Childhood Education International (ACEI)
Childhood Education: Infancy Through Early Adolescence
11141 Georgia Avenue, Suite 200
Wheaton, Maryland 20902

Association for Supervision and Curriculum Development (ASCD)
Educational Leadership
1250 North Pitt Street
Alexandria, Virginia 22314

The Council for Exceptional Children (CEC)
Teaching Exceptional Children
1920 Association Drive
Reston, Virginia 22091

Education Theater Association (ETA)
Dramatics
3368 Central Parkway
Cincinnati, Ohio 45225

International Reading Association (IRA)
The Reading Teacher
800 Barksdale Road
Newark, Delaware 19714

Music Educators National Conference (MENC)
Music Educators Journal
1806 Robert Fulton Drive
Reston, Virginia 22091

National Art Education Association (NAEA)
Art Education
1916 Association Drive
Reston, Virginia 22091

National Association for the Education of
Young Children (NAEYC)
Young Children
1509 16th Street NW
Washington, DC 20036

National Association of Elementary School Principals (NAESP)
Communicator
1615 Duke Street
Alexandria, Virginia 22314

National Center for Restructuring Education, Schools,
and Teaching (NCREST)
Resources for Restructuring
P.O. Box 110
Teachers College, Columbia University
New York, New York 10027

National Council for the Social Studies (NCSS)
Social Education
Social Studies and the Young Learner
3501 Newark Street, NW
Washington, DC 20016

National Council of Supervisors of Mathematics (NCSM)
NCSM Newsletter Leadership in Mathematics Education
P.O. Box 10667
Golden, Colorado 80401

National Council of Teachers of English (NCTE)
Language Arts
Primary Voices K-6
1111 Kenyon Road
Urbana, Illinois 61801

National Council of Teachers of Mathematics (NCTM)
Arithmetic Teacher
Teaching Children Mathematics
1906 Association Drive
Reston, Virginia 22091

National Dance Association (NDA)
Spotlight on Dance
1900 Association Drive
Reston, Virginia 22091

National Science Teachers Association (NSTA)
Science and Children
Science for Children: Resources for Teachers
1840 Wilson Boulevard
Arlington, Virginia 22201

Phi Delta Kappa
Phi Delta Kappan
408 North Union
Bloomington, Indiana 47402

Society for Research in Music Education
Journal for Research in Music Education
c/o Music Educators National Conference
1806 Robert Fulton Drive
Reston, Virginia 22091

The Southern Poverty Law Center
Teaching Tolerance
400 Washington Avenue
Montgomery, Alabama 36104

Teachers of English to Speakers of Other Languages (TESOL)
TESOL Newsletter
1600 Cameron Street, Suite 300
Alexandria, Virginia 22314

Creating Your Classroom **Community**
Lois Bridges
1-57110-049-0   paperback

What do you remember of your own elementary schooling experiences? Chances are the teachers you recall are those who really knew and cared for you as an unique individual with special interests, needs, and experiences. Now, as a teacher with your own classroom and students to care for, you'll want to create a classroom environment that supports each student as an individual while drawing the class together as a thriving learning community.

Lois Bridges offers you the basics of effective elementary school teaching: how to construct a curriculum that focuses not only on what you will teach but how you will teach and evaluate it; how to build a sense of community and responsibility among your students; and how to organize your classroom to support learning and to draw on learning resources from parents and the larger community beyond school.

Math as a Way of Knowing
Susan Ohanian
1-57110-051-2   paperback

Award-winning author Susan Ohanian conducts a lively tour of classrooms around the country where "math time" means stimulating learning experiences. To demonstrate the point that mathematics is an active, ongoing way of perceiving and interacting with the world, she explores teaching mathematical concepts through hands-on activities; writing and talking about what numbers mean; discovering the where and why of math in everyday life; finding that there are often multiple ways to solve the same problem.

Focusing on the NCTM's *Curriculum and Evaluation Standards for School Mathematics*, Susan takes you into classrooms for a firsthand look at exciting ways the standards are implemented through innovative practices. She introduces you to new ways to organize your curriculum and classroom; suggests ways to create meaningful mathematics homework; gives you ideas to connect math across the curriculum; and links the reflective power of writing to support mathematical understanding.

For the nonspecialist in particular, Susan shows that math really is an exciting and powerful tool that students can really understand and apply in their lives.

Music as a Way of Knowing
Nick Page
1-57110-052-0   paperback

Nick Page loves to make and share music with his students, and it's likely that you will too by the time you've finished his passionate, thought-provoking book. You will also have developed a new understanding of and appreciation for the role music can play in supporting learners.

Rich with ideas on how to use music in the classroom, *Music as a Way of Knowing* will appeal especially to classroom teachers who are not musicians, but who enjoy and learn from music and want to use it with their students. Nick provides simple instructions for writing songs, using music to support learning across the curriculum, teaching singing effectively, and identifying good songs to use in the classroom.

He assures you that with time, all students can sing well. And once you've read this book, you'll have the confidence to trust yourself and your students to sing and learn well through the joy and power of music.